Praise for *Brilliant Bu* Creativity

With supreme ability, Richard reveals how the application of a brilliant creative addition can turn any good idea into sheer magic.

Richard French, one of the most creative and mould-breaking figures in British advertising, Founder of French Gold Abbott, FCO and CEO of Young & Rubicam (UK)

Richard provides a wonderfully clear and compelling way to awaken the creativity in each of us. He is 110% correct that creativity is the path to success in today's complex, challenging business environment.

Matthew K McCreight, Robert H. Schaffer & Associates, Managing Partner

Richard's effective tips show how all of us can rediscover creativity and enjoy the thrill that comes with it.

Alex Poracchia, Global Corporate Chief Actuary, Zurich Insurance Company Ltd

Richard has written a book that is fun to read; and I reckon it has gripped a point in an economic cycle and says: creativity is the way forward for all our businesses ...

William Tayleur, Director, Business of Culture Ltd

Refreshing, motivating and simple ... It arrests, questions and challenges you to think beyond your boundaries. A must-read for anyone from entrepreneurs to managers to trainees.

Deepak Vasandani, Founder, Aanya Real Estate

brilliant

business
creativity

What the best business
creatives know, do and say

Richard Hall

Prentice Hall
is an imprint of

Harlow, England • London • New York • Boston • San Francisco • Toronto • Sydney • Singapore • Hong Kong
Tokyo • Seoul • Taipei • New Delhi • Cape Town • Madrid • Mexico City • Amsterdam • Munich • Paris • Milan

PEARSON EDUCATION LIMITED

Edinburgh Gate
Harlow CM20 2JE
Tel: +44 (0)1279 623623
Fax: +44 (0)1279 431059
Website: www.pearsoned.co.uk

First published in Great Britain in 2010

© Pearson Education Limited 2010

The right of Richard Hall to be identified as author of this work has been asserted
by him in accordance with the Copyright, Designs and Patents Act 1988.

ISBN: 978-0-273-73028-6

British Library Cataloguing-in-Publication Data
A catalogue record for this book is available from the British Library

Library of Congress Cataloging-in-Publication Data
Hall, Richard, 1944-
 Brilliant business creativity : what the best business creatives know,
do and say / Richard Hall. -- 1st ed.
   p. cm.
Includes bibliographical references and index.
ISBN 978-0-273-73028-6 (pbk.)
 1. Success in business. 2. Creativity--Economic aspects. I. Title.
HF5386.H2356 2010
650.1--dc22
                            2009041145

10 9 8 7 6 5 4 3 2 1
14 13 12 11 10

Typeset in 10/14pt Plantin by 30
Printed and bound in Great Britain by Henry Ling Ltd., at the Dorset Press,
Dorchester, Dorset

The publisher's policy is to use paper manufactured from sustainable forests.

Contents

About the author

Following a senior career in marketing and advertising, Richard now runs his own consultancy, Richard Hall & Associates, where he has worked with clients as diverse as Heinz, Zurich Financial Services, Nestlé, Royal Bank of Scotland, ING and the Royal Mail. He chairs London's leading presentation consultancy Showcase, a major children's charity Shaftesbury Homes, and Arethusa and the Friends of St Nicholas in Brighton. This is his sixth book; he is published in twenty countries. He lives in Brighton with his wife and two grandsons and two great nieces and families all living close by.

Acknowledgements

In a book on creativity, for heaven's sake, it's reasonable to expect a vague attempt at thanks that are conceived creatively.

Sniff, sniff.

I'm going to cry.

I can't help it.

Sniff, sniff.

I want to thank ...

My mother who bore me.

My father who bored me (well actually, no, he didn't!).

But you see Gwyneth's problem . . .

Writing a book is easy if you have a great team of sensible people who point you in the right direction and hope for the best. And most of all hope you shut up at moments like this.

Mine include Kate (my wife – still my wife despite all this – have you ever lived with a writer? Well ... don't), Sam (my editor – Ingrid Bergman to my Humphrey Bogart), Lucy, Kirsty, Caroline, Richard (great name that ... rolls off the tongue), and, to the whole Pearson team, thank you. Hugs, kisses and, blimey, you're patient.

No one reads these things so (and as Smiley said, what a great 'dead letter box' this is) I can safely disclose the sixth man was Henry Shartpiece . . . which may mean MI6 will ban and pulverise this book which, given how I feel right now, given I missed the Booker, the Whitbread and the bus, would be great.

Creative? How well done would you like it? Bloody . . . ? Yes, I can do that.

Introduction

Beauty and creativity

Many people think creativity is like beauty, something you are blessed with rather than something you can acquire. But beauty can creep up on the unsuspecting and change what in childhood was frankly plain-looking if not downright ugliness (think of Julia Roberts or Sophie Dahl, for examples).

But creativity works in reverse. Nearly all children are creative. They create stories. They don't think within boxes. They play. They have new ideas the whole time and they are very visual.

What happens is we educate creativity out of our young people.

So here's a chance to put it back into them when they need it most – at work.

The pundits' definitions of creativity

Definitions of creativity in the *Oxford English Dictionary* are frankly disappointing. Here are the best:

- 'To form out of nothing'
- 'To be the first to represent a role and so to shape it' (in acting)

In times of doubt I go to Edward de Bono, who always seems blessed with the certainty you'd expect from a man who wrote a book entitled *I am Right and You are Wrong*. He's also been regarded as an authority on creativity ever since he came up with the idea of 'lateral thinking'. Here's what he says: 'The logic of creativity is the logic of patterning systems' ... 'creativity can be defined as the search for alternatives'. In his book *Serious Creativity* he says looking at things in new lights is conducive to getting new ideas. This book is designed to give you, as it were, the creative spectacles that will open your creative eyes again.

Konosuke Matsushita, the founder of Panasonic, said – inspiringly – that he believed managing a business was just as creative as painting a picture. And I agree. Without creativity we will find it hard to get things done nowadays.

My own definition of creativity

The ability to see new ways of doing things and a mindset which rejects conservative thinking. The process of idea generation which makes interesting connections. A restlessness to make new things happen. A belief that the status quo can always be improved and that our role in business is to change things so they become better/cheaper/faster.

Can you teach creativity?

The generally held view has, usually, been 'no'. Either you had it or you hadn't got it. This belief sustains, despite the fact that most of us had creativity in our childhood.

Creativity by some is even seen as a bit flippant and not very grown-up. This view of creativity as childish is really peculiar, and I think it comes from a deep-rooted puritanism: either you were a Roundhead – a real businessperson and a process engineer – or you were a Cavalier – a dilettante, entrepreneur and a bit creative. The trouble was if you were the former you were more likely to be right but were almost certainly rather dull, while if you were the latter you were almost certainly good fun but you probably ended up losing your company millions before you lost your head.

Before people like Michael Ray in the United States and Edward de Bono in the United Kingdom, creativity certainly got a bad press (and it can still do so). Creative accounting was to be avoided at all costs; and now creative financial instruments are seen as worse than sexually transmitted diseases because they can spread contagiously. But concepts such as new business models, change management, product innovation, creative marketing and inspirational management (which by definition will all involve some level of creativity) are now seen as essential. Creativity is being widely used at last.

So can you teach it? Of course you can.

Michael Polanyi, the philosopher, said 'We know more than we know we know' and teaching creativity relies on this fact.

What sort of person are you and in what sort of business?

The too simple definition of Roundheads and Cavaliers nonetheless helps in telling us how likely a person or a business is to be receptive to creativity.

The reality is there will be a scale from left-brain Roundhead to right-brain Cavalier:

Numbers } ←——————→ { Visions

Facts } ←——————→ { Ideas

Targets } { Risk

Being at either extreme is not what anyone ambitious and sane would want.

Neither would we want to be a Mr Gradgrind from Dickens' *Hard Times* ('Now what I want is facts ... facts alone is what's wanted in life') nor could we aspire to be an Einstein who said 'imagination is more important than knowledge'.

Looking at the table below you can begin to decide how you and your company veer. Left or right?

Here's how the characteristics of the two mindsets typically play out.

Roundheads	Cavaliers
Taking out cost	Creating new products
Simple downsizing	A radical new business model
Driving sales	Re-launching the company
Fixing price	Engaging customers
Productivity programmes	Creating a new culture
Focus on margin	Focus on growth
Money	People and skills
Serious	Highly humorous
Finance	Marketing
Business-speak	Emotional language
Safety	The unknown
Profit	Reputation

How you can learn creativity

Creativity can be learned firstly by *opening minds* and spirits so the depth of knowledge, experience and half-remembered connections are mined. It is about releasing suppressed ideas. Secondly by *opening eyes and ears* so we understand the facts of situations and hear the truth. The real skill is to see things as they really are not as we want them to be. Thirdly, as we shall see, there are exercises in virtually everything that can open *our willingness to learn* and improve productivity and perform-ance. The Actor Manager Henslowe in *Shakespeare in Love* when asked why,

> creativity is about releasing suppressed ideas

when things looked really tricky he was so confident they would turn out well, always replied 'I don't know; it's a mystery'. Creativity needn't be and indeed isn't a mystery (added to which chief financial officers, CFOs, the power-men in modern management circles, don't like mysteries).

Creativity is a powerful business tool which helps you find clever solutions to seemingly intractable problems; it's not a muse-driven gift.

Getting out of that wretched 'box'

You will be relieved to hear the expression 'thinking outside the box' will be used only once in this book and that is here. It is of course the commonly used way of describing creative thinking and it's not very helpful, because what is needed in business is *to think within the box, within the rules that have been set by the consumer or the trade or your own corporate guidelines and within that box do something truly unusual or remarkable.*

Even Picasso regarded the confines of the brief as the challenge rather than the challenge being to write a new brief.

My favourite story about creative thinking that really works is from Mick Nash, Managing Director of Sedley Place, the design company. A friend of his who became a client and a col-league was a schoolteacher who was exasperated by the children in his classes constantly leaning backwards on their chairs and overbalancing. It was disruptive and dangerous. In fact around 5000 children a year go to hospital for treatment after falling over backwards and banging their heads. 'Can you solve the problem', he asked Mick, 'by designing a chair that can't over-balance when they lean backwards?' With great gravity (in fact, of course, he was thinking of centre of gravity), Mick said he could. 'Ah', said his friend, 'but here's the really tricky bit – it has to cost less than £20'.

I love Mick's response: 'That's not the tricky bit. It's actually the brief.'

Creativity that business really needs

This book is about achieving the art of the possible. It's about answering the brief. It is not about the 'off-the-wall' absurd idea that we see contestants produce in programmes like *The Apprentice*. Like him or loathe him, that old curmudgeon Sir Alan Sugar (now Lord) has one focus – does it work, does it sell things, do the experts recognise it as being fit-for-the-purpose for which it has been designed? And in fact I've heard him use the word 'creative' approvingly more than once.

The next time someone tells you they have a problem in business, get them to do three things:

- Be totally clear about what the nature of the problem is (sales; profit; cost; growth; market share; new products; product quality; employee relations; investor relations; reputation; customer relations).

- Divide that problem into as many different components as you can and de-bug it as much as you can – in other words assume you can remove the niggly issues which are combining to create one big problem.

- Get a group together to think up as many new ideas as possible to make the problem go away or better still transform into an opportunity (example: we can't meet market demand becomes we *can* increase prices, make a big increase in profit and *control market demand*).

And when they ask you what this is all about, tell them it's 'creative thinking'.

Yes, but I don't know how to do it

'I don't know how to swim.'
'Tough luck then. You're going to drown in modern business.'

Many people when they are asked to come up with some creative ideas say they don't know how to do it. It provokes a similar reaction to someone being asked to swim or walk a tightrope. If that tightrope were only a foot off the ground rather than a hundred feet up they might have a go at it quite fearlessly. All you have to do is focus on how far you have to walk not how far you can fall.

All creative thinking in this book is done a foot from the ground and we also give you a safety net. Because the key message of this book is that *creative thinking is within the capacity of everyone*.

This does not mean that I can help give you a genius creative mind but in my experience people in business generally have more creative talent than they realise. The very least that I can do is give you the equipment to generate useful ideas and have the confidence to participate in creative idea generation.

Reading this book will make you want to try to find new solutions and discover that positive thinking alone is the first confident step along that tightrope. This book can help you stretch your ability and discover that getting your brain to work in uncon-

> getting your brain to work in unconventional ways is stimulating and useful

ventional ways is stimulating and useful. It does not talk about creativity as some mysterious and magical thing. It asserts that it's a tool at which everyone in business must be competent in understanding and confident in using.

The right and the left brain

The right brain as we all know is where intuition and creative-leaps live. The more nerdy left brain is into measurement, maths and minding the shop. But you need both.

What has happened is we moved from being a right-brain civilisation to a left-brain civilisation after the Industrial Revolution. We became supreme engineers. Then as we became a knowledge economy we became very confused. As educationalist Sir Ken Robinson suggests, we may be educating our brains in totally the wrong way for how the world really is and is going to be.

The fact is we are now moving to an ideas economy where we have to be both Roundheads and Cavaliers, both left brain and right brain. Unfortunately if you are a man you are the wrong sex. Women are miles better at the sort of juggling I am talking about. Don't worry – the best companies and teams of the future will have a good mix of men and women and will be able to adapt to the extremes of measuring, analysing, gauging, developing, thinking, taking a creative leap and so on.

What we need are creative men and women, and I believe the huge need for them will mean they'll exist in the next generation, provided that today and henceforth we use our whole brain and are very flexible.

Thinking is the key, not creativity by itself

The word itself – 'creativity' – is what freezes most people in their tracks as it implies doing something which very few people can do – in that respect it's like magic.

Nick Fitzherbert is a magician. He's a member of the Magic Circle. He's also a PR and marketing man and now a teacher of presenting and creative thinking. We'll hear more from Nick later but I love his quote from Lord Saatchi: Maurice says about creative thinking, 'It's the last legal way to gain an unfair advantage.' But we'll gain that advantage by starting with rigorous hard-headed thinking. Until you have thought through all the issues and have created a clear and a logical brief we can forget about trying to be 'creative'.

Only when we know where we are and why we are there can we decide to flex our creative muscles and try to see how we can cost-economically get to where we want to get (note – business creativity should always be about achieving economic as well as effective results).

The most important words in business today are as follows: you must aim to be:

- cheaper
- better
- faster.

If you aren't ticking each one of those boxes then the chances are you aren't thinking hard enough and you certainly aren't thinking creatively enough.

How things have changed

In the good old, bad old days it really wasn't quite so hard. We had jobs for life. Management was simple. People did what they were told. (Alternatively they went out on strike.) This was when the concept of 'management by objectives' was formed – a wholly left-brained world.

But now we live in a global economy where the big broadcast media are fragmenting and failing and where almost anything can happen and constantly does. It's a world where getting employees to do what you want (which 90 per cent of the time is to change the way they work) has never been harder. Ask the guys at the Royal Mail and at British Airways. In such a world we need three things:

- A clarity and conviction about what we stand for.

- A clear vision about and relationship with those whom we are trying to lead or to whom we are trying to sell our products or services.

- The ability to be very flexible and responsive to change.

In modern business, creativity is not a nice-to-have, it's a must-have. *It is the thinking tool which enables change to happen and be made to work and, what is more, be winningly communicated.* Yet research shows fewer than 10 per cent of companies discuss it at Board level.

Creative everything

Our world is more demanding. We are looking for more innovation and increasingly smart solutions. The world of restaurants is awash with creative ideas, not least from chefs like Heston Blumenthal. Quite simply nowadays cooking is a creative art, as is gardening, and if you doubt me go to the Chelsea Flower Show. Dozens of people spend their holidays on creative writing courses. And the criticism of a business or marketing plan that 'it isn't very creative' is tantamount to being told you are a loser.

This book can help you do three things in your job:

- Create ideas and solutions that are fresh, that are different enough, that (above all) work and that are 'outstanding' in the literal sense of that word.

- Have the confidence in your mental equipment to know that you can consistently become a prolific idea-generator.

● Earn the reputation of being a creative 'Mr or Ms Fix-it' with all the potential rewards an image of being creative brings.

Flexing your creative muscles

Above all, this is a practical book that shows you how to improve your creative thinking. Throughout the book there are a series of what I call warm-up exercises, so as you approach the more rigorous gymnastic exercises in the middle of the book you'll be loose enough to coast through them. Here are two to start with:

brilliant warm-up 1

Doodling. Become an elaborate doodler doing tree diagrams, linking words, creating boxes that are linked. Start to think in shapes. Doodle away. It's good for you.

brilliant warm-up 2

Deep breathing. Do it for a few minutes, trying to loosen up your neck, shoulders and hands. Rub your hands together. Stretch. Best of all take a Pilates class and speak to your body. Deep breathing works.

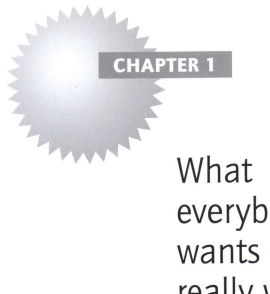

CHAPTER 1

What everybody wants (really, really wants)

I n so competitive a world, where the only way to stay ahead is to improve constantly and to change, the need for creativity is obvious. If we can find clever new ways of staying ahead, we can win. Individually we can out-think other people and make it easier to succeed. And the context in which this creativity will be used is one where bosses, shareholders and customers are all demanding products and services that are delivered faster, better and cheaper.

To whet your creative appetite, this chapter shows how creativity provides the answers to the needs that drive virtually every modern business. Those more able to adapt to circumstances and achieve these needs will do better than their competitors.

The three needs

- The need to do things *faster*. Productivity has been a burning issue for a long time, and globalisation has made it even more important. If you are a slow worker (however accurate) or your service standards are slower than your competitors you are going to lose.

- The need to be *better*. Good enough is not good enough. Tesco Value has been found out – compare meat, fat, salt contents with Aldi and you'll see that Aldi is better quality. Cheaper and worse is no longer an option. Besides which the modern rapacious customer expects to see 'new, improved' and, if they don't, they think the provider isn't trying hard enough. In what author Peter Senge called a 'learning environment' customers expect their provider of product, or services to learn how to improve.

● The need to be *cheaper*. The old-fashioned premium price school is looking out of date now. Expect many prices to come down. Even select places like McKinsey will get cheaper because of market pressures. Martin Broughton, the ex-President of the CBI, said before he left that CEO wages in the United Kingdom were too high. He might have added that so too are prices. No longer will the United Kingdom be called Treasure Island by people exporting goods and services to us.

Something else also matters: trust.

---

brilliant example

Jack Welch, who used to be boss of GE, had very clear views about what really mattered in business. The value he added to the business during his stewardship proved he was right. He said this towards the end of his office: 'Stop worrying about technology. Start worrying about who trusts you.'

Faster

The world is moving faster. The need for speed is obvious if you want to keep up let alone get ahead. Creativity is about finding time-saving ways of working. Creativity is a great tool for finding short cuts.

Create the right structures where everyone knows what they are doing and why. One of the ways of slowing a business down is to lack organisational clarity. In the film *Patton,* the US army in the Desert War is a shambles. Patton stumbles over a sleeping soldier who apologises. Patton, for once, is saying gently: 'You know, son, you are the only person round here who seems to know what they are doing.' Clarity makes you do things faster.

brilliant tip

From BMW to whom design is a religion and for whom building a brilliant brand enables them to get paid more for the metal they shape, a word on why it pays to speed up . . . 'The big do not always eat the little. The fast always eat the slow.'

An example of a creative structure is Google where everyone is in teams, focused on specific and understood tasks and they are managed with a light touch. Be intensely customer-focused and try to exceed expectations when it comes to delivery. The management technique Six Sigma showed that minimising variation of delivery time was the secret of better performance. If you promise something in two days, getting it to your customer in a day and a half is great. Getting it there in half a day is as bad as being a day late. Jack Welch, the former chairman of General Electric and an early adopter of the technique, said: 'We reduced delivery span from 135 days to 2 and got stuff to customers closer to their want dates.' (Or, as they saw it, faster.)

Tell people the truth. Do not over-promise and under-deliver. Tom Peters, co-author of the best-selling book *In Search of Excellence*, is the most influential and cantankerous business thinker of today. He claims that airlines are slow and lazy and that airline pilots were all 'congenital liars' and, indeed, mendacity was a prerequisite for the job. Lying slows things down.

Coach people so they work out how to do things faster. Too few people learn the short cuts in life, the ones that make all the difference. Are we sharing all the good stuff we learn with those around us?

brilliant timesaver

When you're facing a long 'to-do' list and the last thing you feel is creative, get some momentum going. Do all the tasks that can be got out of the way quickly, first. You'll find releasing time also releases a bit more capacity to be creative.

Have you got the right staff? Are these the sort of people capable of getting faster at what they do? We put up with bad behaviour because the people have been there a long time or because callously removing them seems a bit medieval ('off with their heads!') but having the wrong people in the wrong job is a recipe for being slower and worse: it's a brake on creativity.

Create a crisis and see how everyone reacts. The management consultancy R.H. Schaffer and Associates, in the United States, do this and find that people tend to rally round in a most impressive way. They cite the story of snow in northern Georgia in 1993 which, being so heavy, made a factory roof collapse, immobilising one of the two production lines at the Mohawk Carpet Mill. The employees and management got the remaining line producing what both had been producing within days of the disaster rather than the predicted weeks.

simplification is the quickest way of getting faster

Re-engineer your processes and logistics. Can you simplify what you are doing? Simplification is the quickest way of getting faster. Ask Bose. Ask the people who do the work, don't just impose this. Get them to work out how to do things faster without compromising quality and see what they come up with on their own.

⤴ brilliant exercise

Get half a dozen people together in a circle, give them three tennis balls and ask them to pass them to everyone in the group with both hands of each person touching each ball; do it as quickly as possible with a repeatable and effective technique. How quickly? About 1 or 2 seconds is your goal. And it can be done (see below for the answer* and then use this at an off-site meeting).

Outsourcing might be an answer if you can find people who'll be quicker at the particular exercise than you'll ever be. Good freelancers can also be an answer. Think of the film crew on a James Bond film – outsourced freelancers every one of them. And why do they go to Marc Wolf of Flying Pictures to do the aerial shots? Because he's better and, critically, he works faster than other people.

Think 24/7/365 because that's the way the world is and you'll have to match that speed to survive. Read *The 24 Hour Society* by Leon Kreitzman to discover the service stations on the motorways and 24-hour Asdas may be the paradigm for the future, a world where clubs in Brighton stay open all night, which has extended to libraries: Bath University, for instance, now has a 24-hour library.

Better

If you aren't trying to improve what you make or the service you provide, be it Coca-Cola, Heinz Tomato Ketchup or your own office supply company, you have stopped being creative. Creative is not special. It's what you do when you try to improve.

*Answer: *Think your way to speed.* The answer to the exercise is for the group to stand together creating a funnel with their hands down which the balls are dropped. Creative? Fast!

But the first thing is to compare yourself critically with your key competitors. Next, talk to your customers and listen to what they have to say about your product or service. Do it yourself; do not employ a research company which will simply get in the way.

> listen to what your customers have to say about your product

But that isn't enough. As Professor Keith Goffin of Cranfield Management School said recently, 'most forms of market research are old fashioned or ask the wrong questions'. To be sure we have to listen to what our customers tell us but we also have to observe how they use our product or service and establish the order of priority of things that matter to them.

Find out what you aren't giving your customers that they want and what you are giving them that they don't really need. That's how Toyota discovered the need for a solar panel on the roof of their cars to power the air conditioning when the engine was turned off and drivers wanted a quick, comfortable snooze.

Forget money for a moment. We need to ask ourselves, assuming money was no object, what the perfect product or service in our sector would be like. Imagining the perfect milk chocolate lay behind the creation of the new Green & Black's milkier milk chocolate – filling a taste gap between the existing white, milk and dark bars.

How important is what the world in general thinks about us apart from primary users? Do people say, 'wow, you've got a Canon PIXMAR MP780 printer. Impressive!' But if there's a chance to turn people on in this way what would accomplish this? Apple does it. Sony does it. Harley Davidson does it. Maserati, with its Quattroporte S, does it. Joseph does it in its fashion stores.

How important is innovation … the ability to tell people you've done something new or made a significant improvement? Talk to the Marketing Director of Honda and it's rather like listening to a recently seen-the-light evangelical minister. Innovation is in Honda's very DNA.

Apple's Steve Jobs believes passionately in simplifying things and taking unneeded choices away from the consumer. He says, 'As technology becomes more complex, Apple's core strength of knowing how to make very sophisticated technology comprehensible to mere mortals, is in even greater demand.' Research has shown that nearly half the technological products returned as being defective are in fact in perfect working order ... they are simply too difficult for people to figure out.

↗ brilliant do's and don'ts

KISS: Keep It Simple, Stupid. Simplicity beats complexity every time. Simplify your offering so it is easier to use and understand. Think Aga, think Apple. Think what you can leave out to make it easier to use. Apply simplification to everything you do – everything. Doing less, not more, is very creative.

Listen to all stakeholders, not just your customers. A negative comment by a journalist or retailer can do untold damage to you. Companies such as DAV and publisher VRL run frequent 'roundtables' to discover what the business communities that touch their business – customers, observers, influencers – think about what's going on. 'What's on your mind right now?' is a pretty good question.

You have to get out into the real world. You can't be creative sitting in your office. You have to get out there in the streets where your customers are.

Youth matters more than ever. So make sure you understand how younger or more junior users perceive and use your offering as opposed to your more mature users. When it comes to mobile phones this is critical. That's why technically well-informed young men are so hopeless at selling products to ageing technophobes. I went into a T-Mobile store to ask if they had a charger for my two-year-old Nokia and the smooth young man laughed at me and said, 'Blimey – haven't seen one of those for ages. Museum piece that.'

Cheaper

For many the accepted wisdom used to be that if a product cost more – that it was premium priced – then it was also, by definition, better. The past tense 'was' is used because of globalisation. What we all need to do is create ways of delivering great product and service at lower cost than before. Nowadays Michelin star restaurants in London are doing two course lunches for £10. This is what I'd call creative pricing.

We are always told to avoid the word 'cheap' and, instead, to use the words 'good value'. I've never agreed with this. 'Good and cheap' is a great place to own. The Lidls of this world are now using dump-bins in their stores announcing, 'hey, that's cheap!!' Shamelessly effective.

Simplification is the double whammy. It improves the customer experience (see above) and it reduces cost. That was how the Biro was born. Do not over-engineer. Giving a TV extended life so that it outlives its owner is unnecessary; a car in which parts have wildly different life and performance expectations is wastefully designed; a £24 vacuum cleaner from Asda might last just two years – which is fine.

The more you make the more you save. It's how Asda and Tesco manage to get more price leverage, although how Walmart almost killed the gherkin market by promoting the gallon jar at $9.90 is a salutary story of going too far. Once half America owned a gallon jar of gherkins the demand for the things tailed off and the market had gherkin-saturation or indigestion.

Dynamic pricing is a concept triumphantly exploited in the airline industry by companies such as EasyJet. In other sectors the Easy brand uses it with less conviction. EasyPizza is cheaper if you order it a week earlier than if you order it for immediate delivery (in an impulse-purchase market that's strange thinking). However, in principle the idea is great. There are medical units around now that offer discount prices on MRI scans if you come at less popular times of the day. The mission is to fully utilise the gear. Good thinking.

The creative use of raw materials can also make a difference. Go to the eco-friendly and green blog search engine Keetsa and look for the Terra Firma clutch bag and tote bag made from discarded sweet wrappers (http://keetsa.com/blog/recycle/sweet-bags-made-from-wrapper/). Actually, they're not so cheap but ordinarily the wrappers would have gone to landfill. The bags look fabulous by the way. Or that man Mick Nash, from Sedley Place, again who has worked out he can have those school chairs that you can't turn over by rocking back on them, from old school chairs. One hundred per cent recycling. Brilliant creativity.

Costs can also be reduced by creative new methods of employment. David Neeleman, ex-CEO of the airline JetBlue, created what he called 'home-sourcing' whereby 400 reservation agents worked from home. They were cheaper to employ and gave a better service partly because they love where they work. Less well-paid staff (either younger or older or people who find it hard to get jobs) can be employed: well managed and put in the right roles, this can work absolutely brilliantly. B&Q do this with their staff of retired shop workers. They are practical, courteous and tend to be very well informed.

Good management is the key. So too is good training. It's amazing how good training can inspire people, improve performance and productivity, and save cost. Finally, a question about how to reduce costs. The most creative thing that happens when asked to reduce costs is to employ the most creative punctuation mark of all – ? The question mark. Ask whether every part of the process is necessary or whether what is being done could be done another way.

The problem of deterring graffiti artists in New York was considered insuperable until the authorities hired teams of their own painters. The 'vandals' stopped bothering to target the subway with graffiti when their artistry was immediately painted over. Zero tolerance – zero graffiti. Money saved in the long run – a creative solution to a social irritant.

---

brilliant example

Heinz constantly work out how to make perfectly strong cans using a fraction of the steel they used to use. The money saved can be re-invested in marketing keeping them ahead. Never stop trying to save money, especially on things like packaging as opposed to key ingredients. Always seek out ways of being cleverer. Saving money is creative – that's the real point.

Click: the light bulb of understanding goes on

An insurance company was trying to improve the way it operated, looking for operational efficiencies and bottom line impact. The underwriters couldn't cope with the workload as they were being asked to make too many quotations yet the request for more staff was rejected. Result: they had a badly performing, de-motivated, operationally defective business.

The CEO met the underwriters. He asked a few questions:

- How many quotes are we producing?
- How many turn into business?
- How many brokers are we dealing with?
- Who are the brokers who give us most business and who are those who give us none?

They discovered that over a long period of time 10 per cent of the brokers who constantly asked for quotes seldom produced any business. 'Why?' he asked. 'Go and ask them.' Get them to give us business or stop giving them quotations which were clearly being used as a 'stalking horse'. The choice was simple – free up 10 per cent of time (or increase business by selling more policies and being able to afford more staff).

The light bulb flickered. Another bit of creative brilliance.

The answer nearly always becomes clear when you analyse the activity that is being generated and how much of it converts to money.

So don't accept the status quo – go and ask questions – data drives everything and you have to fish where the fish are and where they are most hungry. The real impact of this story is the culture began to change and people at the front line who actually did the work felt empowered to ask more questions and began to allocate their time more productively. They felt more in control.

How creative is this? *Anything that shifts the status quo is creative.*

But go back to what I said about 'thinking'. Whenever the brain starts working creativity isn't far behind. This story is about emancipating the creative potential of a workforce. It's hard to get more creative than that. Anyway I just love the click, click, click of intellectual light switches.

brilliant warm-up 3

Let your eyes go 'soft'. Stare at the horizon, focusing on nothing and let your eyes wander aimlessly. The point of this creative warm-up, a little like the last one, but this is more intense, is to empty the mind of chatter and stuff and be ready for something better. Soft eyes = hard thinking.

brilliant recap

- You need to be faster because you'll be eaten alive if you aren't. The slowest fish get eaten first.

- You need to be better because customers expect to see 'new, improved' not 'old, the same-as'.

- You need to be cheaper because in a crowded, global economy you have to compete on price. C. Michael Armstrong, former Chairman of AT&T, said that 'unless you are (price) competitive all other issues are moot'.

- The extent to which your customers trust you is key to your success.

CHAPTER 2

What we say about creativity and what we actually want in real life

t's time to reflect for a moment. You can't spend every second doing creative gymnastics. This chapter is about reconciling the way companies talk about creativity and the way they behave towards it. It's about asking you to ask yourself if your company is of a size, mindset or skillset to be creative. Bear in mind creativity involves hard work and hard thinking.

Our whole educational system is hostile to creativity – more a case of the three 'Rs' than three 'Aahs' – more about being clever than being smart and effective. But by remaining cool and keeping the creative banner flying we can move the game on and make ourselves more inventive and more creative, and we'd better do it if we want to remain competitive as individuals, as companies and as a country. By now you are getting increasingly accomplished as a creative thinker – this chapter is the springboard for the next two which will take you to mastery of the creative process.

From innovation course to boardroom

We've constantly seen it. People go on a creativity course and come back from it really inspired. Creativity immediately goes top of their agenda. No one's wearing a tie any more. There are high-fives going on. Words like 'breakthrough thought' are constantly heard. Idea generation meetings fill diaries. New briefs are given to agencies. Mission statements are rewritten.

But then there's a blip in sales and it looks as if 'the number' (that's the budget) is going to be missed in Q3. Suddenly all the feathered hats get put away and the round helmets get taken out and polished. Costs are cut, salespeople are put on extra commission, a price promotion is announced, the agency budgets are cut and creativity is filed under 'nice to have'.

Everything is back to normal.

↗ brilliant do's and don'ts

Don't abandon using your creative minds when it gets tough. Tough times are when thinking cleverly is really useful. Do spend more time applying techniques which solve your problems. Creativity is not a soft option.

When push comes to shove everything comes second to 'the number'. CEOs and their executives are paid to deliver shareholder value not creative value, to generate ROI (return on investment), not to speculate.

What we want from leaders

Professor Chris Bones from the Henley School of Management talks about a piece of research done in 1990 and again in 2005. It asked people at work what they wanted from their leaders and showed the following:

- 1990: Leaders who are hardworking and charismatic.
- 2005: Leaders who have integrity and consistency.

A bit of a surprise these; nothing of the alpha male competitiveness that Tom Peters likes so much or Jim Collins' Level 5 qualities (Jim Collins, author of books such as *Built to Last* and

Good to Great, defines five levels of management – see Chapter 3 for more). These are soft rather than hard values. I might have expected to see 'profit focused', 'market astute' or even 'deeply skilled'. But worse and more surprisingly there is not a sniff here of people wanting creativity from their leaders. No cry for the driving force that keeps a company alive. What they seem to want is what you'd want from a junior manager, not from a leader in a changing and traumatic world. Welcome to the Mediocrity Party.

Consistency? Integrity? Aren't these basic don't-have-these-and-so-don't-bother-to-apply characteristics? Yet if you asked whether 'creativity' mattered I bet it would go up to the top of the list.

brilliant tip

You have to keep reminding people how cost-effective and helpful creativity is because the trouble with creativity is it is forgotten until you give people a nudge.

Creativity is hot (and getting hotter)

Professor Amin Rajan, no less (former advisor to the UK government and expert on the subject of leadership), in defining corporate drivers of success defines five, one of which is a 'culture of innovation'. In a world changing as rapidly as ours he says innovation is the entry price to survival.

Yet it is more than just an entrepreneurial spirit of inventiveness. Creativity is a cultural phenomenon which can transform a business from a 'no-but' to 'yes-and' enterprise (and how much I prefer *that* word, 'enterprise', to business or firm). But in sheer practical terms creativity is (while no magical tool) like a magician's wand when you are in trouble. Creativity can help you be smarter and more nimble. *It can help you think your way out of trouble.*

Tony Blair, described by Ann Treneman of *The Times* as 'that class act', put creative thinking squarely at the centre of the world stage when he said that 'we are going to see the world economy dominated by the exploitation of creative minds'. Dominated is, obviously, a big word, much bigger than influenced or impacted, words much more likely to have been used by a cautious statesman. Creative minds are headline news. So pay attention. Gerard Lyons of the *Sunday Times* said 'we need to reinvent ourselves and invest in innovation to compete in the emerging markets'. I think Gerard could have gone a stage further and said 'we need to do this *just* to survive'. It's that crucial. Unless you are creative you won't survive. Now do you get it? Yet the United Kingdom languishes at 24th in the world competitiveness tables, this despite Andrew Scott, a professor at the London Business School, describing us as having a 'very flexible and creative workforce'.

The key to what has to happen – which is no less than a *creative revolution* – can occur only if we are smarter about how we play the game of presenting creativity.

brilliant timesaver

To ensure that the creative process is right up your company agenda keep on quoting these figures and this national need. That'll get creativity on the Board agenda faster than anything else. Intriguingly the danger of falling behind is a more powerful motivator than the promise of moving ahead.

How to play the game

The key to succeeding in the corporate world is not to wear your creativity too flamboyantly. No Hawaiian shirts. No tequila sunrises for breakfast. No theatrical gestures. No air kisses. No, it's time to act more like a spreadsheet. Cool. Creativity gets short shrift from the *Harvard Business Review* gurus like Jim Collins, Kim and Mauborgne and Rosabeth Moss Kanter although the daddy of them all, uber-strategist Michael Porter, concedes that creativity in scenario planning can aid strategic development. Just don't run naked down the corridor screaming 'Eureka!'. Be more restrained, like that advertising genius Ed McCabe who said: 'There's nothing new under the sun but there's always a better way.' Can we privately, here and now, agree that this is our mission statement? Our job is to find a better way.

Why big and creative are north and south poles

brilliant example

Creativity doesn't only lie in smart new ideas. It can actually lie in process too. Guess who proves this point? Apple are creative for sure but their greatest creativity today lies in logistics. In 2007 AMR Research named Apple as number 2 in the world (after Nokia) for supply chain management and performance (Apple beat Wal-Mart and Toyota).

So we've started with the exception that proves the rule. But generally whilst big companies know that their long-term fate lies in innovation, they also know that the process skills in developing those ideas tend to staunch creativity. They know the most creative minds will be in the Thames Valley or Brighton and not in Milton Keynes.

What big companies proclaim	But what's in their DNA?
I want creativity	I want profit
I want alpha minds	I want obedience
I want crazy ideas	I want efficiency
I want innovation	I want cost reduction

A.G. Laffley, who ran P&G and is still Chairman, said in 2003 he wanted to outsource 50 per cent of the company's innovation, fast. He'd completely understood the management dilemma about creating great products. It's the corporate oil versus the creative water problem.

Anecdotally we all know that creativity thrives in small tribes. Factually we know that big organisations stamp on difference of attitude. The story of IBM (when in its plume) was of blue-suited, white-shirted, red-tied executives singing from the same song sheet.

In Japan, while they sang the company song every morning, they managed some pretty creative stuff too. In advertising and journalism in Soho they used to go to the pub – now it's non-stop work. In China they went to the photocopier because they agreed with Picasso: 'Amateurs borrow, professionals steal.'

Change and creativity

There is very strong evidence that in times of turmoil creativity flourishes.

Life in Elizabethan England was not exactly like being on a Caribbean cruise and the middle of the nineteenth century was a period of social turmoil, yet look at the creative output from both these periods.

brilliant definition

Where does creativity flower best? Creativity does not flourish in big companies. It belongs where systems and attitudes are more informal with smaller teams that are lightly managed. Alternatively it flourishes in an enterprise where it is proclaimed as fundamental like Apple or where creativity is the *raison d'être* like a small advertising agency. Creativity dislikes the corporate soil where safety first and bureaucratic process apply.

We are now undergoing our own Black Death in economic terms (but like that plague, it will pass). The world will change and we'll try to create a better one, come what may.

Remarkably, the collapse of the unsinkable General Motors is at least as seismic an event as Britain losing its empire. It was Edwin Wilson (ex-GM President) who said 'what's good for the country was good for GM and vice versa'. Not any more.

Quietly, but with determination, we creative spirits have to carry on helping reinvent our lives and find better ways of doing what we do – faster, better and cheaper.

How to survive as a creative person in the twenty-first century

There are a few important lessons.

- **Be cool**. Do not demonstrate your ability to have new ideas too ostentatiously. (Green glasses, purple suits, orange iPods, bare feet and whatever are not a great idea – well, you know what I mean.)

- **Like-minded helps**. Try to work in a creative environment – if you don't you'll begin to lose that creative knack. The

best creative atmosphere is found in small groups like
skunkworks. (A skunkworks project typically is developed by
a small, loosely structured group who research and develop
a project primarily for the sake of innovation.) It was by
hiving off the development of the PC that the mighty and,
by definition, uncreative IBM managed to create the PC.
Under the direction of Don Estridge a tight team of
engineers and designers in Boca Raton, Florida managed to
create it quickly and brilliantly.

- **Language matters**. Use the terms 'pragmatic creativity'
  and 'change management' a lot. Say that business creativity
  is a process not a thing of hunch, intuition and guesswork.
  Never imply it is a gift and a mystery; had you done that in
  the Middle Ages they'd have burned you at the stake. Some
  say little has changed. Positive language also matters. Our
  biggest problems will tend to be around clarity and force of
  communication. Creativity is seldom in pastel colours. Try
  to 'up' the power of your expression.

- **Set ambitious targets** in things to fix, targets to surpass
  and the timescale in which to do them. Deadlines often
  provoke a solution rather than creating stress. Creative
  minds tend to be ambitious to achieve results.

- **Do not take anything at face value**. Professor Allan
  Snyder's work indicated two things about creative people:
  - they tended to be rather late developers academically;
  - they also tended to be rather rebellious. Don't be shy of
    being a little rebellious. That way you get to test and
    question the status quo and open doors to new ideas.

- **Be a bit difficult**. Ask lots of questions if you must – that's
  fine. Stick with it and follow the advice of Gabriel Garcia
  Marquez that the journey is better than the destination:
  'I have learned that everyone wants to live on the peak of the
  mountain without knowing that the real happiness is in how
  it is scaled.'

Enjoy the adventure. Enjoy the climb. Most of all enjoy the happiness.

brilliant warm-up 4

Routine is the easiest way of killing creativity; 'same-as' is death to originality. So change your routine regularly (routinely!) by getting up at different times, going to work by different routes, by avoiding going about in a predictable daze.

brilliant recap

- Creativity courses are inspiring but it takes one crisis or blip back at work for all those mind-stretching exercises to be forgotten and a return to spreadsheets.
- Most people in business exploit situations rather than explore new opportunities. Decide which you'd prefer.
- Creative minds are good at making change happen and thinking their way out of trouble.
- Britain is 24th in world competitiveness tables. Enough said. Not creative enough.

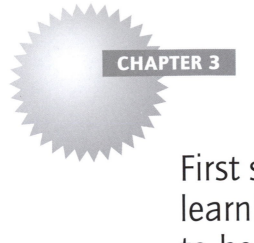

CHAPTER 3

First steps in
learning how
to be creative
in business

n this chapter I'll give the key tool of business creativity – the ability and urge to ask penetrating questions. You'll begin to ask the questions which allow you to see what choices might exist in a business. They will enable you to make an informed journey around a given business which will then allow you to produce an intelligent brief. Here you begin to understand the fact that creative thinking is something informed by data, knowledge and understanding. It is a process. It can be learnt. And it is rigorous.

OK, what's the secret?

There *is* a creative process which after a while becomes second nature. The real creative people – copywriters, artists and poets – may shiver with horror at the word 'process' and scan the sky for the sacred, creative muse but in business there isn't a muse. You stand or fall by your ability to put distance and distinction between you and your competitors. And you need to go through a simple informative process to condition your mind to be relevantly creative, which starts with a lot of basic groundwork.

Some down-to-earth questions

Before trying to be clever, try to be smart. Depictions of business in TV drama or on reality shows are usually of successful businesspeople operating solely on intuition and by hunch. But it's not really like that. Ultimately business and its challenges are rooted in the way people behave, and to discover what's going on you need to become an interrogator. You need to get smart.

Why, why, why?

- What is (or are) the issue (issues) that need solving?
- Why is this issue a particular problem?
- How does it manifest itself?
- What would be the tangible benefit if it were solved?
- Is it endemic or a one-off?
- Has it been going on for a long time?
- What is the story of the people near to the issue who can help me understand the issue better?
- What are the obstacles to solving it?
- Are these internal?
- Or are they external?
- If the product or the service were a person what would it say.

brilliant tip

Imagine the product or service is in the dock and you are counsel for the prosecution brutally interrogating it. Now switch and imagine you are counsel for the defence. Seeing it from both viewpoints will be instructive. That's just so much more dynamic a way of doing a SWOT (strengths, weaknesses, opportunities and threats) analysis which is otherwise known as death by a thousand yawns.

- What in short is the brief?
- What do we need to know in coming up with a solution?
- Who are the stakeholders who need to be covered off?

brilliant timesaver

You can waste a lot of time if you don't know where you are going. So the most important thing is to be absolutely clear what the brief is before you do anything else.

Light bulb time – questions that provoke creative answers

Here is a simple checklist of the various elements that make up any organisation. The challenge in taking a creative view of solving any problem or of taking the business forward is to scrutinise each category and ask searching questions but most of all questions which challenge us to take a creative position.

brilliant exercise

Think about how you could operate *differently enough* to achieve a real, measurable improvement? What would that feel like? A big change or a few simple adjustments?

By dividing the brief into simple components and thinking about how we could do things differently, what Hercule Poirot would have called 'the little grey cells' are taken for a good jog and the process of applying creative thinking can begin.

A creative interrogator's checklist and how to use it

This exercise is about looking at various aspects of a business to see how they could operate differently and what the impact of change would be. The creative aspect of it is that it forces you to ask questions and examine options; moving the chess pieces around as it were. Do this and you'll discover more about a business than you could ever imagine. Better still your creativity will be inspired, provided that you are positive. Look for good aspects that can be accentuated. Look for answers, not for more problems.

> ask questions and examine options; moving the chess pieces around

People

People are the most important and difficult ingredients in any organisation. Great people can make an organisation rock and, if so inclined, they can also bring it to its knees. Professor Ben Bryant of IMD, incidentally, said that 'it's insanity to try and achieve alignment in a business because people are different'. He's right. The most creative insight any manager can make is that you are dealing with lots of different opinions and prejudices when you deal with people. The second most creative is that most people respond to creative ideas.

> great people can make an organisation rock

Processes

Do processes work? Do you have a completely repeatable system of behaviour which says 'when x happens we do y'? Mazda Cars, based in Hiroshima in Japan, operated a very tight 'just in time' process with just under a day's parts in stock. In Hiroshima they have hurricanes. I asked what effect this had if the trucks carrying spare parts couldn't get through. Answer:

we stop the line and everyone sets to tidying and redecorating the factory. Creative solution to natural problem.

Products

It will sound obvious but are your products good enough? Weight Watchers from Heinz introduced a range of Ready Prepared Frozen Meals. To their astonishment the Salmon Mornay was far and away the best seller. The reason was it was by far the best tasting and distinctive product. A creative insight that once stated seems so obvious is that most business failures come about because of product inferiority.

Creativity is inspired by sampling, testing and constantly asking questions about product. The more you get to know a product the better you can see its strengths and weaknesses and therefore what needs changing. That insight is creative.

> creativity is inspired by sampling, testing and constantly asking questions about product

Product portfolio

Do you have too many products? Is your portfolio (as most are) a proof of the Pareto principle with 80 per cent of the sales coming from 20 per cent of the portfolio? Can you simplify your offering and increase your profit? When Steve Jobs was re-installed back from the wilderness (having been removed from office years before) and with Apple now in huge trouble, he simplified the product offering from lots of products to just four. And he re-introduced what he called the missing ingredient at Apple – sex appeal. Jobs said of the Mac OS X's user interface, 'we made the buttons on the screen look so good you want to lick them'.

The most useful creative technique is to simplify things and put your eggs in fewer baskets. Editing is a creative business. Less is more.

Positioning

What are you telling people about your brand? Is it compelling? British Airways was powerful in the 1980s with that wonderfully proud line 'the world's favourite airline'. This was based on fact – more people flew with them than any other airline. So how can you create a proud positioning for your business? What are your biggest assets? How are you different? Do you do anything more than your competitors? Is there something in the way you behave or make your product that is different?

⏏ brilliant do's and don'ts

Do think and think and think. Don't be lazy and stop looking out for distinctions. No two 'anythings' are exactly the same unless they come from the same production line. Everyone and everything has something special or remarkable about them.

Presence

How could you increase your share of mind with all your customers? Think of Avis when they claimed they were number 2 behind Hertz (in fact they were about number 5). That was why they tried harder. Brilliant. (Incidentally, the campaign failed in research and Bill Bernbach, founder of the legendary American creative advertising agency Doyle Dale Bernbach, responsible for this advertising, immortally retorted 'get some other research'. (Bill was famous for his quotes, another of which was 'Logic and over-analysis can immobilize and sterilize ideas. It's like love – the more you analyze it, the faster it disappears.' The sheer confidence of creativity like this can be compelling.) The creative insight of acting in such a way as to inspire people is smart – by, for instance, behaving as though you were cleverer, better looking, more knowledgeable, more experienced, luckier, more skilled or more creative. Confidence is a friend of creativity.

Promotion

Are you spending too much or too little on marketing? The fact that 'creative ideas' save money is because 'creative ideas' get more attention. 'Pedestrian' is expensive. Are you asking the right people if you move them? Do what Stuart Rose did when he joined M&S: he talked to Women's Institutes to see what intuitively he believed (and research confirmed) were his greatest allies and staunchest critics. Creativity is not an absolute. Whatever you do can be described as successfully creative only if it moves the people you want to move.

Channels of distribution

Could you transform your business by changing the route to market, for example by firing your retail salesforce and going through wholesale or by doing exactly vice versa? Or would you be better off selling direct? Direct Line was the pioneer of selling insurance direct and are now a huge, successful business. The creative question here is could you operate differently and make a more successful business? You have to explore all the options dispassionately.

Pricing

Are you price competitive? Could you increase prices? Or should you reduce them? Should you try dynamic pricing? The Factory Direct Malls in the United States in places such as Manchester Vermont work brilliantly because you get half-price Armani, Gucci and other luxury brands. Creative pricing is something street traders or market traders in the city understand brilliantly. People who can sense wafer-thin margins – that, for instance, $\frac{1}{2}$ per cent of a billion is £5 million without thinking. Price is something to play with, for instance, by changing pack size or price per hour or price per unit of distance.

Structures

Do you have the right internal structures? Some believe the key roles you have to get right are CEO (leadership); CFO (money); HR – head of human resources (people). The last is especially important in terms of 'casting' the right people and conducting inevitable downsizing. Most businesses have too many people and they discover just how overcrowded they are when the bad times come. Creative thinking comes into its own when people try to manage a shrinking business.

Culture

Are you happy with your culture and values? How would you change them? Culture is the whole range of values, beliefs, rituals, stories, behaviour and manners you see in a given organisation. The combination of culture, cockiness and confidence that Nike, Google and Apple have is infectious – it impacts on all they do. But the creative bit is in how they express it and how they leverage it. They know who and what they are. They have intense self-belief.

As Janet Lowe (author of *Google Speaks: Secrets of the World's Greatest Billionaire Entrepreneurs, Sergey Brin and Larry Page*) says: 'The values that drive Google's founders ... have created a culture that fosters creativity and fun, while at the same time, keeping Google at the forefront of technology through large, relentless R&D investments and imaginative partnerships with organizations such as NASA.'

Strategy

Do you know where you want to get? In a single sentence write this down. Great strategies are those like Aldi, Pret a Manger, Barclays and Green & Blacks (I've never seen such fast and convincing line extensions as theirs). Creative strategies happen (as we shall see) when we acquire the self-confidence and insight to predict the scenario in which we are likely to be operating in the future. Great strategy is clear about the destination it is trying to reach and how it will get there in broad terms.

Tactics

Tactics are the precise modes of transport to get us to our strategic destination. Question: how good is this business at execution? ('Good ideas are common; what's uncommon is someone who will work hard enough to bring them about', John Westerby of *The Times*.) Social networks are now a catalyst in promoting speed of response. Domino Pizzas had an instructive catastrophe. Two employees mucked around in their kitchens putting cheese up their noses and so on, then filmed it on their mobiles and put it on YouTube. Millions saw it. The pizza, as it were, hit the fan. No one at Domino watched YouTube and when told about it presumed 'it would all blow over'. It didn't.

Leadership

Are you well led, inspiringly led, strongly led? Can you lead? Chances are one day you'll have to. Leaders need to be great communicators like Charlie Mayfield (Chairman and Chief Executive of the John Lewis Partnership). Being a compelling leader requires creative thinking. It seldom requires being stuck in a big office terrifying those who work for you. Great leaders are seldom like Alan Sugar. Jim Collins, in his book *Good to Great*, defines five levels of people in a business that are any good (presumably Level 0 is a not very effective individual):

- Level 1 - highly capable individual
- Level 2 – contributing team member
- Level 3 – competent manager
- Level 4 – effective leader
- Level 5 – Level 5 executive

Customers

What is your relationship with customers? How could you improve this? Do you *really* know what they collectively think you need to improve or change? Companies such as Nestlé and Heinz do. Sophisticated businesses don't think flying without radar leads to creativity. They think it leads to crashes. Creativity is aided by how much you know about what your customers know, feel, do and think they might do next. Creativity teaches us to take no one and nothing for granted – ever.

Competitors

Do you know who they are? Do you know what they are better at or worse at than you? Do you know what they think of you? Tesco told us something really useful. They accelerated ahead of Sainsburys when and only when they began to focus on their own performance and their own values. In other words their creativity flourished when they worried about how good they really were rather than how good they were relatively. I wonder if they still remember that.

Knowledge

Is there a deep pool of market and customer understanding in the business? The people with the best market understanding, the best products and the best memories will usually win. *Creativity is rooted in robust data, not whim.*

Now what do you do with all this?

Well simply by going through the checklist you've thought really deeply. You'll have a mass of unrelated ideas in your head. It's time for practical actions.

> ### brilliant tip
>
> 'Taking the first logical step towards completing a task relieves people of much of the worry of things undone and clears the mind to allow creative thinking' (David Allen in his book 'Getting Things Done').

Getting things started

These are the questions you need to resolve, practical not esoteric questions. The word 'questions' appears more than 'answers' in this book because the most creative process you can indulge in is that of curiosity. The sort of curiosity Einstein had.

Creativity is not meant to be fancy, it's there to make something change. It's a tool not an ornament. This is not a book about creativity in general. It's about business creativity specifically, and to that end we need to clear our mental desks before we start that long, hard process of thinking.

> **creativity is there to make something change**

> ### brilliant warm-up 5
>
> Use stimuli to inspire and energise you. Mobilise the senses. Eat raw carrots to give you energy. Listen to your most energetic music to give you courage, like the best Western or film music ever. Experience great smells like freesia and the great taste of Coke (or whatever it is that personally turns you on). Warm up your creative instincts by relaxing your body.

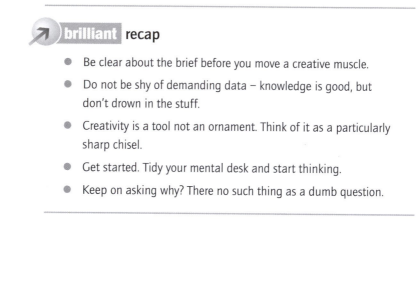

brilliant recap

- Be clear about the brief before you move a creative muscle.

- Do not be shy of demanding data – knowledge is good, but don't drown in the stuff.

- Creativity is a tool not an ornament. Think of it as a particularly sharp chisel.

- Get started. Tidy your mental desk and start thinking.

- Keep on asking why? There no such thing as a dumb question.

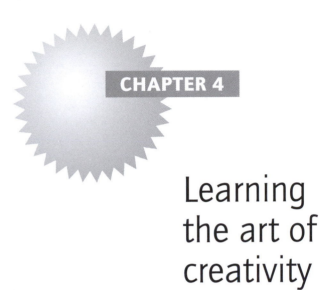

CHAPTER 4

Learning the art of creativity

The real art of creativity in business lies in making connections, in cross-referencing ideas so you start to think in a more supple way and see things differently. Creativity is about being relaxed enough to generate lots of ideas, not just one great one. And then the real art lies in getting rid of the rubbish.

This chapter equips you with some basic but powerful creative tools which will get your mind in the right place and focus your creative instincts.

brilliant do's and don'ts

Don't simply unthinkingly surrender yourself to your right-brain intuition but never, ever ignore your gut. Listen to it. Hear what your inner voice is saying (you may have 500 reasons to do something but if your heart isn't saying 'yes' don't do it).

Professor Allan Snyder from Australia and Director of Centre for the Mind, in his book *What Makes a Champion?*, says two interesting things:

● 'Any company or corporation is only as good as its next big idea: and creativity is the driving force that incubates these

big ideas.' Thinking of 'creativity' as a driving force stresses
the power that many people see in it. Imagine a company
devoid of creativity and you are looking at a place potentially
about to die.

● 'Studies have shown that child prodigies ... rarely amount to
anything [... with exceptions like Mozart]. What is really
important is learning how to struggle, how to recover from
adversity and how to adapt ... I arranged for Nelson
Mandela and a group of 50–60 extraordinary people to be
together ... what I discovered was that creativity is an act of
rebellion. To be creative, you have to confront conventional
wisdom; you have to break with convention.'

One further point – very often the best companies take a while
to mature too. Sam Walton took a long time getting the Walmart
model right. It was worth waiting.

often the best
companies take a while
to mature

So what are some of the most
important secrets to the conditions
in which your creative thinking can
flourish?

Your willingness to be subversive

Snyder's anecdote about Nelson Mandela intrigues me.
Realistically you don't have to be behind an actual revolution
but you do have to have the balls to say 'no' to what seems
wrong or stupid. You are not a lemming. I went on an offsite
meeting in Switzerland with the advertising and marketing
group WCRS. We had a series of group creative games at one
point. One, facilitated by an American couple who were world
famous at this stuff, comprised making as many small white
houses as you could in half an hour out of cardboard card. Our
group revolted because it seemed so silly. We made an enormous
house out of white card with white card Ferraris and Porsches in
the drive. The facilitators told us we were a disgrace and this had

never happened before and, just wait for it – 'the other teams will hate you. They will deride you.' The reverse happened. Everyone wanted to be in our team. They applauded us. The facilitators were booed and fled the meeting.

brilliant tip

If you are not willing to ask questions to the point of being subversive, you won't be creative. Because creativity involves breaking rules; business creativity is about breaking rules but be careful, it's not about breaking businesses. Say what you really think, go with your gut, don't be frightened. If something feels wrong to you, you are probably right.

Your state of mind

Are you relaxed and receptive? Are you comfortable in your shoes? Are you excited by the prospect of discovery? Are you deeply interested in what's going on around you? Einstein, who will be mentioned from time to time in this book (in any book on creativity he has a big share of the market in ideas), said: 'I am neither especially clever nor especially gifted, I am only very, very curious.'

brilliant tip

Do you wonder why young children ask 'why' so often? It's because they are curious and their creativity is waiting to be ignited. So be curious about everything. Curiosity is the oxygen of creativity.

Understanding complexity

Paradox and confusion lie at the centre of the modern world and anyone who demands black and white solutions is going to be unhappy. If complexity can be unravelled it needs especially open and receptive minds and an ability to juggle thoughts and issues. Complexity leads to creativity because it makes you really use your brain.

> complexity leads to creativity because it makes you really use your brain

Any answer may be the right one

Do not try to bend the evidence to prove a point. Be open-minded and prepare to be very surprised at the answer you might get. Dogma and a determination to be right will impede your being creative. Changing your mind is not a crime. As John Maynard Keynes said: 'When circumstances change, I change my mind. What do you do?' Remember creative thinking can lead you to surprising places. That's why it's so powerful.

More is more

Do not be lulled into thinking one idea will do. Fecundity of ideas gives you the chance to select and to refine. The trouble with having only one idea is it presupposes that you are infallible. You aren't. Einstein said once he'd only had a couple of decent ideas in his life. I suspect that he had an endless stream of good thoughts and that Nobel Prize Winner Linus Pauling is being more honest: 'The best way to have good ideas is to have lots of ideas.'

Team beats solo

Creativity is seldom a solitary pursuit (except when it comes to maths, poetry or composing music). If you are to create a great business ideas machine you have to be very skilled at getting the best out of those around you. Encourage them to be full of 'let's try' and 'could we?' and 'what if?'. The impressive innovation company based in Marylebone, incidentally, call themselves ?What If! and in their book *Sticky Wisdom: How to Start a Creative Revolution at Work* they describe the key to a creative team being to 'source a wider diet, seek out new experiences and ways of thinking about their market, products and internal processes ... the new perspectives they gain provoke them into making *creative connections that others won't have made*'.

Creative connections are the root of creativity. Here's an example: Yotel. The rooms were designed to be small but luxurious. How do you achieve that? By asking the designer of BA First Class to do it. He understands space limitations brilliantly. More recently ?What If! have launched 'Skinny Innovation' for the straitened economic times in which we live. It's about being creative on a budgetary diet. Having creative insights calls for brainpower, radical thinking and bravery – not lots of money.

brilliant timesaver

Often it seems quicker to do it yourself than sit in a team getting frustrated because the others don't seem so much on the ball as you'd like. The reality is working in a team is almost always going to get you from A to B *quicker* and better than flying solo.

Diversity is the key

You need to have a mixed group in your team if you are to have truly breakthrough thoughts. Here's what G. Pascal Zachary (author, teacher and scholar) said about diversity in the *Wall Street Journal*: 'Diversity spawns creativity, nourishes the human spirit, spurs economic growth and empowers nations.' *That's terrific because it drills to the core of what makes the human race so adaptable.*

Research has shown too that a diverse group will always be better at creative problem solving than a group of like-minded, similar people, however clever they are.

Yes, do make me laugh

Don't underestimate the power of humour, it is one of the most creative tools there is. Most humour relies on a shift in dimension or the creation of a new connection or the simple surprise that an unexpected ending can have. Many jokes like many great inventions or discoveries are so obvious when they are delivered, yet still somehow unforeseen.

---

brilliant example

A professor stood before his philosophy class and had some items in front of him. When the class began, he wordlessly picked up a very large and empty mayonnaise jar and proceeded to fill it with golf balls. He then asked the students if the jar was full. They agreed that it was.

The professor then picked up a box of pebbles and poured them into the jar. He shook the jar lightly. The pebbles rolled into the open areas between the golf balls. He then asked the students again if the jar was full. They agreed it was.

The professor next picked up a box of sand and poured it into the jar. Of course, the sand filled up everything else. He asked once more if the jar was full. The students responded with a unanimous 'yes'.

The professor then produced two beers from under the table and poured the entire contents into the jar, effectively filling the empty space between the sand. The students laughed.

'Now,' said the professor as the laughter subsided, 'I want you to recognise that this jar represents your life. The golf balls are the important things – your family, your children, your health, your friends and your favourite passions – and if everything else was lost and only they remained, your life would still be full. The pebbles are the other things that matter like your job, your house and your car. The sand is everything else – the small stuff.

'If you put the sand into the jar first,' he continued, 'there is no room for the pebbles or the golf balls. The same goes for life. If you spend all your time and energy on the small stuff you will never have room for the things that are important to you. Pay attention to the things that are critical to your happiness. Spend time with your children. Spend time with your parents. Visit with grandparents. Take time to get medical checkups. Take your spouse out to dinner. Play another 18 holes. There will always be time to clean the house and fix the disposal of garbage. Take care of the golf balls first – the things that really matter. Set your priorities. The rest is just sand.'

One of the students raised her hand and inquired what the beer represented. The professor smiled and said, 'I'm glad you asked. The beer just shows you that no matter how full your life may seem, there's always room for a couple of beers with a friend.'

Do not underestimate the importance of *surprise* in creative thinking … that moment where logic *seems* to go out of the window and a 'creative leap' takes place.

brilliant tip

'The great thing about listening to someone with a sense of humour is you listen extra hard in case they say something funny' (Baroness Trumpington).

See what you mean

Practise deep imagination and develop the power of visualising what things might be like in different circumstances. Trying to imagine what brand leadership would feel like might lead you to discover that it feels like having a superior product to the competition (not a blinding insight to be sure but it might re-focus you on what is needed). Also being able to imagine yourself in a different place experiencing all the sensations of smell, taste, sound, touch and sight is enormously powerful when you do it.

Dream on

Dreams are even more powerful if you can get them to work for you. Just because you are asleep doesn't mean your computer is turned off. Try two things before you go to sleep.

● Put all the issues you are struggling with into a metaphorical box and imagine locking it.

● As you are going off to sleep imagine what it might feel like having solved your problem in a brilliantly creative way. I've tried that and dreamt of the solution. Kekulé was allegedly a dreamer whose dreams resolved both the molecular structure of benezene and how carbon atoms link to each other – although there is doubt as to whether this is true. True or not, it suggests that many believe in the power of the brain to make great leaps while its owner is asleep. So dream on ... letting your mind roam free while you sleep may be surprisingly productive.

If you can't explain it, it's got a flaw

Great creativity is always capable of being rationalised. 'It's green because it's green' is not a compelling argument. Do not imagine the random, off-the-wall piece of 'inspiration' will cut any ice with an investor. In pragmatic creativity there may be leaps and breakthroughs but it can always be explained in the same way an accomplished critic can deconstruct a painting or a poem. If a 'creative' idea is inexplicable or illogical, it isn't creative, it's silly. Don't be hooked by fairy dust. An idea may transcend logic but if it seems daft it probably is daft.

The enemies of creativity

If you want stamp out creativity at work here's how:

- Create a state of fear – which given the way so many companies are run means this has become a prevalent issue. People who are in fear of losing their job or apprehensive about the reaction of their peers, may (in their view wisely) have decided to keep their head down. But this is a rotten posture from which to attempt creative thinking.

- Create stress – a frisson of adrenalin is fine but the disabling strain of anxiety brought on by over-work is alien to that calm and patient feeling that the 'waiting creative mind' should feel. Stress is an enemy to almost anything worthwhile. If you feel it, stop what you are doing, have a beer, go for a walk, anything just to keep it at bay.

- Distraction – the discipline of creative thinking requires concentration and focus. Don't try to do it while fiddling with your Blackberry because people with short attention spans will seldom be much good as creative thinkers.

- A lack of cooperation – if those around you are frightened of creativity or don't want to try and think creatively it makes the generation of new ideas really difficult. But there's one obstacle much worse than passive indifference and that is ...

- Active cynicism – when you are with a bunch of people who simply don't believe in the creative adventure there is little you can do (in fact just one person with the wrong attitude can stymie you). Given that murdering them is possibly an over-extreme option, the best way forward is to politely suggest to the cynic that they get lost or better still you must drive them away before they make you into one because cynicism is very infectious.

↗ brilliant do's and don'ts

Don't commit murder but do get rid of negative thinkers before they corrode the group you are working with.

- Bureaucracy – small companies are usually much more creative than big ones where hierarchy and a process-focused way of working will usually be anti-open-minded. The bijou perfection of a Ben & Jerry, Pret a Manger and Innocent are all creative successes and now sold in total or in part to larger businesses. We'll see what happens now but I'm still hopeful. Because small companies will get very stressed in an economic downturn and in such a climate, creativity (when it is most needed) can tend to be suppressed. That's not so likely if you have a sugar daddy and aren't fretting about short-term issues.

We need more good ideas

I loved the concept of sell-by dates as a way of driving sales volume – 'Mr Sell-By' is responsible for consuming more food in my house than anyone else. But I also love the idea that everyone at work has a sell-by date.

brilliant definition

Would you define yourself as being part of the problem or a contributor to the solution? After five years of innovation and change in a business, a brilliant performer stopped being a problem-solver and started being part of the problem. So you've got to stay fresh. No choice. Because everyone has their sell-by date.

Unless we retain our inventiveness and focus on product improvement, speed of delivery and cost reduction then we are doomed. But I am an optimist and think it's going to be just fine, as does Steve Jobs, who is quoted in the fascinating book by Leander Kahney *Inside Steve's Brain* as saying 'the people crazy enough to think they can change the world are the ones that do it'.

Where does Apple's innovation come from? Kahney is clear it is rooted in attention to detail: 'Like any complex phenomenon, it comes from many places, but much of it from Jobs' careful attention ... he is alert to every aspect of the customer experience. His instinct for the experience of using his products is what drives and informs Apple's innovation.' We may not become a Steve Jobs, but by practice and application to some basic principles we can begin to share some of his creative vision.

brilliant warm-up 6

Do a map on a big piece of paper of where you've been, what you've done, what you know, whom you know, what you've learned and where you want to go next. You'll fill the sheet. It'll make you feel very confident and strengthen your self-conviction. (Don't do it as a list. Put it in boxes, in circles with interconnecting arrows and so on. Have some fun.)

↗ brilliant recap

- Listen to your gut – it's a good friend to judgement.

- You have to be a bit of a rebel to get that creative force going. Yes-men are seldom creative.

- You have to be in an unstressed, receptive, positive mood to be at your creative best.

- We live in confused and paradoxical times. You have to get used to this and learn to juggle.

- The best way to have good ideas is to have lots of ideas and work in a team. Solo heroes are history.

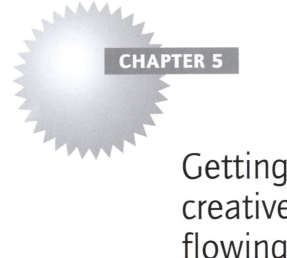

CHAPTER 5

Getting your
creative juices
flowing

This chapter is about how to prepare for creative thinking. Too many people in business are under-prepared. They 'busk' meetings. They don't have a desired outcome in mind. Creativity is the last thing in or on their mind.

I'll take you through some warm-up exercises, ones you've seen at the end of chapters so far and some new ones, to help you relax and prepare your mind for creative thinking. I'll also show you how to build your self-belief and self-awareness so you can let yourself go and truly embrace creativity, how to break routines so you are exposed to new influences to spark tonnes of creative ideas, how to see above detail to come up with 'big' ideas, and, finally, how to take all of this one step further.

The importance of warming up

Whether running a race, singing in a concert, playing golf, taking an examination or flying a plane, the process of 'warming up' so that when you start, you are loosened up and ready to be at your alert best, would certainly be seen as sensible by everyone. So don't expect to be creative when you are hungry, stressed, travel-weary and unprepared.

> don't expect to be creative when you are hungry, stressed, travel-weary and unprepared

Yet many of us arrive on the first tee still aching from the stressful drive in the car; we do a couple of swift practice shots and then hack the first shot into a bush. Or, even worse, we play a blinder, think 'hey, this is my day' and by the time we've reached the ball in the middle of the fairway we can't remember what we did 250 yards back or how we did it. Our confidence and self-belief crumbles. It's going to be a bad day.

My task is to help you understand how to access your creativity consistently and then be able to do it again and again with a repeatable, creative swing.

Getting your mind ready to think

Here are a series of stress-removing exercises which are fundamental to warming up.

Doodling

Something happens when you scribble some random thoughts onto a piece of paper. Think about a problem you want to solve, something clear like, say, 'how to increase sales'. Spend five minutes loose-doodling.

Sales ⟶ *number of salesmen* ⟶ *distribution channels* ⟶
levels of distribution ⟶ *customer satisfaction* ⟶ *product*
comparison with competition ⟶ *pricing* ⟶ *packaging* ⟶
customer service ⟶ *after-sales* ⟶ *why do people buy?* ⟶
why stay loyal? ⟶ *is it high on their radar?* ⟶ *who's doing well?*
⟶ *what do people say is going on?* ⟶ *what is going on?*
⟶ *is there a big idea lurking?* ⟶ *a transformational /*
paradigm-changing idea ⟶ *biggest, best, cheapest, fastest, slowest,*
cleverest, easiest, smartest, safest, coolest and on ⟶ *what's the best*
we could expect? ⟶ *what's stopping us?* ⟶ *imagine a winning*
streak – what would that take ⟶ *change*

Use words, squares, arrows, pictures, anything you feel like. Downloading your thoughts clears your mind and ignites your creative thinking. Doodles can be italic (*doodle*), bold (**doodle**), numeric (123456) or even graphics (R♥K) ... just let yourself go.

Deep breathing

Do it for a few minutes trying to loosen up your neck, shoulders and hands. Rub your hands together. Stretch. Best of all take a Pilates class and speak to your body. But deep breathing is always good.

Use soft eyes

They help you become passively observant. Stare dreamily at a whole scene without focusing on anything in particular. Let things come to you rather than you trying to organise what you see. (As Lao Tsu, the ancient Chinese philosopher and central figure in Taoism, said: 'The world is ruled by letting things take their course.') Enjoy being still, yet still alert. Avoid that fidgety, uneasy state that characterises today's world; flashes of 'I should have done ...'. Let ideas float into your head.

Increase your energy levels

Carrots – the quickest release of blood sugars you can achieve, or if you prefer them, Mars Bars, Red Bull, a banana.

Creativity needs to be fed with sleep, energy and plenty of 'feel good'. Explore ways to achieve all three in the best way for you. I'm not worried about the calories; I'm very worried about the inspiration you'll need and can get.

brilliant timesaver

Use whatever changes your state fastest – that's why the good old carrot is such a favourite. The trick is to know what works for you in stimulating you to feel like a creative work-out.

Prepare your mind

Creativity is made easier by four states of mind:

- having a blank mind;
- being very relaxed;
- being hungry to do something (not famished for food);
- having the right kind of mood (such as believing that creativity is a wonderful thing).

Change your mood

You need to feel *positive*. Find stimuli to change the way you feel, if your mood is low. These will tend to be personal and to some extent to depend on taste. For me music always does the trick:

- Powerful and 'assertive' music (mostly from films): *The Magnificent Seven*, *The Man from Laramie*, *The Big Country*, *633 Squadron*, *The Great Escape*, *The Dirty Dozen*, *Patton*, the friendship duet from Verdi's *Don Carlos*, Beatles' 'Eight Days a Week', *Lord of the Rings*, *The Godfather*, Clapton's 'Layla', etc.

- Sentimental music (or what I call HR music): *An Officer and a Gentleman*, *Pretty Woman*, *Working Girl*, Carly Simon's 'You're So Vain', anything from *La Traviata*, Bernstein's 'Somewhere', Cher's 'Gypsies, Tramps and Thieves', the friendship duet from *The Pearl Fishers*.

- Intellectual arousal music: Mozart, especially the chamber music. Sir Paul Robertson, leader of the Medici String Quartet, who also teaches music, has done a lot of work with autistic children and has shown that Mozart's music has a particularly beneficial effect on their behaviour because of its intricate note patterning. Bach does something similar – great music to write to – soothing, sensible, sensitive. Others that do this for me in the classical sphere are Mahler and Stravinski and also a lot of jazz.

You choose the music that does it for you. And while you are about it, choose the eight Desert Island discs that define who *you* think *you* are, because in a complicated world which can be quite political, you want to stay true to your values. Music is a useful kind of 'psychological glue' which reminds you of what it feels like being where you want to be and of what you stand for. Control your mood through music which moves you or which you love. Use it to lift you just when you need it.

How to be open and ready for creativity

We are what we think we are. We either, like Ronald Reagan, are comfortable in our own shoes or, like others of us, not very comfortable at all. But having a decent sense of self-perception is going to help in grounding us before we try flying in creative circles. It's only when you know who you are that you can let go. As Paul Michael, one-time employee of Charles Schwab, said: 'I'm creative when I simply let go of my preconceived notion of who I am and just let myself be.'

Be true to your beliefs but learn to lose your ego: 'Be what you is not what you ain't 'cos if you ain't what you is you is what you ain't' (Luther B. King).

By pinning down your core values and being dispassionate, you'll get new creative impetus and energy. Your ego slows you down. Try the following: map what you are, what you've done, what you know, who you know, the list of the most important influences on you, the most amazing places you've visited, the best things you've done. After this, define your single key strength.

Most of us totally underestimate what we've done, where we've been and the contacts we have. Start to change that.

> most of us totally underestimate what we've done

And don't be influenced by what others say.

brilliant tip

If people tell you you are wonderful or not so wonderful or that you have skills or the reverse, take it all with a pinch of salt and don't get too fussed by it. Some of the greatest people have been told they aren't going to make it (Robin Cousins by a new coach, the Beatles by Decca). Some of the least successful or those who created the greatest disasters believed they were great. Believing what others want you to believe is a big obstacle to creative thinking.

Use history to help – we live in the present, not in the past, but what you've done and where you've come from can be helpful in shaping the way you frame your thoughts and may provide clues as to the strongest influences on you. This could very easily be a teacher or a sports coach. Getting into the right frame of mind can be massively helped by recollecting previous triumphs or moments when you felt in really great form.

brilliant tip

Focus on what makes you remarkable ... not what you think you are good at. This will involve asking others what they think about you. Do it.

Routines – break them!

If we always do everything the same way how can we ever expect to achieve anything different? Einstein claimed that behaving with that particular mindset led nowhere but to insanity. The idea is to create a shift in perception caused by mildly different behaviour which in turn allows you to see things in a new way.

Change your work routine

Get in late, leave early or get in very early and leave at lunchtime. Try to parcel up work into 'just getting stuff done' and 'really making something valuable and different happen'.

Change your play routines

Get out of the 'every morning I go for a run' mindset. Start to surprise yourself by being a bit of a rebel or perhaps, less threateningly, an individual who is their own person. Stay in bed late occasionally. Go for a long walk, a really long one. Do something you've never done before. Shift the paradigm and see what happens after a month.

brilliant tip

Unchanging day-in-day-out routine destroys supple thinking. From time to time try to find ways of shaking yourself up … different shop, different paper, different dress code.

Walk different routes

Walk where you've never been before, where you have to concentrate. See how many different things you can see.

Change your form of transport

When did you go on the top of a bus, travel in a stretch limousine, ride a bicycle or a motorbike, or go in a hot air balloon? Just try seeing things from a different perspective by doing things differently. In a tube strike in London once I remember being vexed to find I had to walk a mile to an appointment but it turned out to be through St James's Park in a very slight drizzle and it was absolutely wonderful ... cornucopia of ducks and trees and flowers and tourists and a bizarre sight – a man taking a ferret for a walk on a lead.

Do something out of character

Bart Sayle, the ex-Unilever anthropologist turned creative guru, demonstrated the point when on a creative workshop he was running he sang 'Danny Boy' powerfully and almost in tune to prove what getting out of your comfort zone was like.

Try selling stuff in the street. Try acting. Try busking.

The thinking behind all these is to push yourself into a zone of discomfort because, for sure, all creative thinking will, by definition, take you to a new place.

Getting above the detail

Elsewhere I've argued against 'stabs in the dark' as a sound creative methodology, that attention to robust data is required to produce a business solution that is pragmatic and buyable by others. But as well as delving deep among the trees we also have to see the wood as a whole. In short we have to get above the detail. We do that by two techniques.

- **Mentally walking the 'shop'.** This means thinking about what a given business feels like – where are the customers, where are the pressure points, what feels hot, what feels cold, what feels right, what jars, what feels as though it has potential and yet is underperforming?

brilliant definition

Lucid dreaming. The process whereby you envisage every single detail, smell, sound, sight of a potential experience. Start every other sentence with 'Imagine that ...'. Lucid dreaming allows you to steer your imagination broadly where you want it and still create surprising unthought-of surprises.

- **Seeing things from other viewpoints.** How would your mother see the issue you are dealing with – how would you describe it so she could clearly understand it? Do the same for a 9-year-old, a journalist versed in your business sector and finally a competitor. Oddly our competitors are often more astute at seeing our challenges and how they could be solved.

Exercising our eyes, minds and powers of observation

What I've discussed and suggested trying will start to make an important difference. You'll be curious, thinking differently, change your view. Most importantly you'll move your mind around a problem to see it from different viewpoints.

> move your mind around a problem to see it from different viewpoints

To help take this forward try some real experiences relevant to your own market which will give you anecdotes, new things, new thoughts, conversations, anything which sparks off new ideas.

The market

So whatever your marketplace, go there and see what is happening. If it's fast-moving consumer goods, walk around a couple of supermarkets watching and listening.

If you're in B2B go to a trade show, or wherever it is that you can sense what is going on in your market. Talk to a wholesaler, an architect, a specifier, a journalist, a consultant or a customer.

By talking to people and looking into the whites of their eyes you begin to work out what is going on and discover the key issues on their agenda.

Human beings

Whether we are selling ice cream or plastic cans, perfume or photocopiers the human interaction is what counts – *how people respond to other people and to different situations.* The magic of business creativity is that it can, like real magic, capture people's imagination and change the way they think and behave.

All creatively minded people in business that I know are pretty good 'people-watchers'. So you should be too. It helps you get ideas and it makes you more observant.

Learn how to sink into the background and become a passive observer of the way people behave. (And, by the way, people-watching and voyeurism are not the same thing.)

The pre-flight check for getting ready to take off on a creative-thinking flight is very important and avoids your taking unnecessary risks. Choose some of these exercises that work for you and rigorously go through them before you embark on a group creativity programme.

There is no inconsistency in suggesting under 'breaking your routine' that you should be systematically unsystematic. The whole essence of creative thinking is that you create the process that works best for you as an individual within which your lively mind can have unusually interesting thoughts and ideas.

Now it's time to get more ambitious.

brilliant warm-up 7

Lie down and think about what you've taken from this chapter. What are the exercises that work best for you? Imagine trying the best three of them ... and imagine what it would feel like. See if you can see and think about something new and different. This is 'lucid dreaming'.

🡕 brilliant recap

- Your warm-up exercises and what I call 'pre-flight check' are important if you want to be at your thinking best creatively.

- There are a large number of easy to-do exercises from doodling to watching with 'soft eyes' to getting in the right mood, using music (for instance).

- Use good moments in the past (and how they felt) to guide you to good feelings about now.

- Change your habits and routine every so often so you shift focus on the way you see things and think about them.

- Learn how to dream lucidly by, for instance, imagining you are walking around your business seeing what really goes on.

CHAPTER 6

Applying creativity

You are beginning to doodle, be a bit of a rebel, become very observant and curious about how things work (your partner went barmy when they found you'd completely disassembled the vacuum cleaner to see how it operated – never mind it still works, almost perfectly apart from that strange whining sound).

You are talking about creativity and have become interested in advertisements and new products. Your memory has improved. You spend a lot of time wondering if you could do your job better and if so specifically how and where.

'If you say "why?" one more time I'll leave you!' your partner said the other night. Mmm. There could be compensations to this creativity business. But you wonder if you are good enough yet. Don't worry; as Henry Van Dyke (the late nineteenth/early twentieth-century author, educator and clergy man) said, 'Use what talents you possess. The woods would be very silent if no birds sang there except those who sang best.'

Now that you're feeling creative, this chapter shows you how to take the next crucial steps in applying your creativity in the workplace.

Step one: See things not just from different viewpoints, but in radically different ways

How did a company that one might have thought as being one of the more conservative-thinking companies, Nestlé, create such interesting products with such unusual routes to market as Nespresso and Skinny Cow? (www.skinnycow.co.uk)

Distributing the former direct – so it always arrives with you in great condition and is relatively affordable – and the latter launched in George and Topshop, where it was sampled with brilliant accuracy to its target market, were acts of fresh creative thinking. Someone at Nestlé had had the courage to work out a better way of doing things.

brilliant tip

Finding a better way of doing things is a pretty good, simple way of describing what matters most in creative thinking in business. Creative is different, better and clever.

- **Flexibility**. Have the flexibility to find a different way of doing things. If you are going to be creative don't decide before you've thought about it what the answer is. Look at the options. Take your time. Never start a sentence 'obviously …' because very little is obvious. There are usually several solutions and not just one.

- **Focus**. Yes, focus on the brief. Sit with a large pad and write down the brief and anything that comes into your head. Download thoughts. Connect words. Shortage – drought – famine. They may not (at first sight) make sense but what you are doing is letting your brain have freedom to express. Relax. Enjoy yourself. But try to stay focused on that brief.

- **Alignment.** To many people good meetings are about agreement. Many of us want to be liked. In being creative we must be good natured but clear about what we really think. Alignment matters less than healthy challenge, debate and the generation of ideas. Remember Mark Twain on wanting to have consensus:

> While a Consensus was proving, by statistics and things, that a steamship could not cross the Atlantic, a steamship did it. A Consensus consisting of all the medical experts in Great Britain made fun of Jenner and inoculation. A Consensus consisting of all the medical experts in France made fun of the stethoscope. A Consensus of all the medical experts in Germany made fun of that young doctor (his name? forgotten by all but doctors, now, revered by doctors alone) who discovered and abolished the cause of that awful disease, puerperal fever; made fun of him, reviled him, hunted him, persecuted him, broke his heart, killed him. Electric telegraph, Atlantic cable, telephone, all 'toys', of no practical value – verdict of the Consensuses. Geology, paleontology, evolution – all brushed into space by a Consensus of theological experts.

Step two: Turn things on their head

Try looking at a market or a situation in a different way. By doing that you may see a solution that you'd miss if you simply look at it at face value. Imagine you could change things. Imagine you could remove a competitor. Imagine what the very best things could be. The key word here is *imagine*. For example:

- What would happen if your product was free?
- What would happen if you had to join a club to get something like Nespresso?
- How could you get more people to try your product?

- How could you get your people to work harder?
- Could you simplify the way things work in your business?
- Why don't you take more holidays? What would happen if you did?
- What would happen if you stripped out most of the activity with which you are involved and focused on just a few things? Think two years downstream not in the immediate future.
- What would happen if you sold your product only over the web or, alternatively, if you set up your own exclusive retail outlet and sold it there?
- How price sensitive is your product? What could you do to it which would justify a premium price? What would happen if you reduced the price? If you can find legitimate ways of increasing your margin then you are going to make your boss and the shareholders very happy people.
- Imagine you were operating in a completely different market where the rules and processes are distinctive – what would change? Consider the different processes for four different markets. What would happen if you transposed them?

Step three: Learn from other market dynamics not old paradigms

Look at markets as though they were other markets – why is food sold in supermarkets and clothes in department stores? Why have Asda and Tesco changed this paradigm?

Try this creative exercise to see how creativity can change the way you look at things. Use your imagination to improve how things might work.

brilliant exercise

- Imagine we applied some of the more protracted dealer contact relationships to food – suppose we could build a 'what would you like from us next?' relationship.
- Suppose we could have our clothes 'serviced' at a low cost – buttons replaced, stitching adrift and so on – or suppose we could trade them in.
- Suppose we built an on-going relationship between customer and shop or website so that a transaction became the first step on a lifetime relationship. What would it need to do this convincingly?
- Suppose we made car showrooms places where everyone could get to play with and understand all the technological toys in a car … suppose we were to target the juvenile 'pesterers' whose power and capacity to understand technology we all recognise.
- Suppose people who used Amazon or Tesco online were asked what they wanted rather than being told what they'd like, proving thereby a beady eye has been kept on their past purchases. The way in which the database is used could be more sensitive and interactive; more involving and less didactic. We know these companies are clever – they shouldn't show off. My research says they are getting this wrong at present most of the time.

brilliant do's and don'ts

Do listen to your customers. Do respond to them. Don't present yourself as omniscient – it puts people off. Remember the Betty Crocker Cake Mix story. The brand failed until they gave the consumer something to do as well … 'just add an egg'.

go to the desired
solution and work out
how you might get there

If thinking the way you normally think isn't proving productive do it a different way. Go to the desired solution and work out how you might get there by, literally, thinking backwards.

Step four: A magic way of thinking

It's Nick Fitzherbert's idea, he of the Magic Circle. It's what magicians do. They go to where they want to get from where they are and work out in reverse how they got there. Here's an example of that in practice.

Result: We improved productivity by 25 per cent and reduced waste to insignificant levels.

How?

↓

3rd milestone – all usable waste recycled back into production.

↓

2nd milestone – production workers asked to work out how to reduce the number of people working on this process.

↓

1st milestone – get everyone together to see how to increase productivity of line A – crude reward: a big night out together if we can achieve 20 per cent saving – emphasis 'no one's job at risk'. Front line workers sort it out.

↓

Problem: productivity on line A needs improving and waste needs reducing which would produce a big profit improvement.

It's a fact of life that if you think of where you want to go, your brain and instincts will tend to take you there. Visualise the destination and not the journey.

> visualise the destination and not the journey

The force of creativity is that it can help you move things and change them. And the one thing that everyone wants to change are those irritating glitches in a workplace that stop it working properly, from relatively trivial things such as a light bulb not working, a defective photocopier, a person who's always late, a supplier who always pays late to sporadic product quality problems to an excess of internal emails. These are the bugs.

Step five: Eliminate the bugs

One of the most destructive forces that impede creative thinking is being distracted or frustrated by things happening in the business or in one's working life; things that constantly seem to go wrong. These bugs in the system are a pain. Sit down and write out a list of all the bugs that need removing. Work out the simplest way of removing the bugs because these are the obstacles to you thinking creatively. Examples:

- Overrun by emails and voice mail? Transfer all the emails from one PC to another then delete the lot so you can truthfully say 'I transferred them to my other PC and lost the lot – if urgent please re-send'. Or change your phone number. Or just wipe the lot. Plead insanity, drunkenness, your small child or sabotage but do not let a few emails ruin your life. When my PC went down a while back people said to me 'how ghastly, I'm so sorry' as though someone close to me had died. They seemed surprised when I said I was finding it very liberating.

- Your team are not helping each other. You don't have to be team leader to fix a chat over a few beers on the topic 'how can we work better together?'

- Untidy office. When I'm working, my office gets progressively more untidy until I can bear it no more and have to go on a blitz of tidying up. Then I feel so much better and clearer.

Banish the bugs. Then you can start thinking positively and creatively.

Step six: Lubricate your mind

Creativity does not happen spontaneously. It needs to be provoked by something that creates – in effect, a thinking-domino effect. If *y* happened then *x* could happen and then *z* and bingo! To achieve that impetus you need to binge on stuff that stimulates you. For example I talked about going shopping and using your eyes. Also try the following.

> creativity does not happen spontaneously; it needs to be provoked

- Magazines – buy a lot and a box of chocolates. Have a pair of scissors with you to cut out anything you feel like.

- The *Sun* – read by more people than any other paper apart from the *News of the World*.

- *The Times* and *Guardian* – look for funny stories – oddball things that make you laugh.

- *The Week*. Good fun. Quick read.

- The best of current YouTube.

- The most interesting websites you can find – surf lazily, seeing if you can find some interesting ones that make you think about new things – look under 'creative', 'different', 'life-changing'.

- Read a comic – get back into visual stimulus.
- Splash some colours on a board and see what happens. Start painting again.
- Listen to some of your favourite music.
- Read a book you've always meant to read.

Then go for a very long walk alone or do some gardening – digging is good and pruning even better; activities where part of the mind is focused and concentrated and the rest is swinging free in a kind of intellectual hammock – resting, reflecting and wondering. This process is about filling the brain with fresh, different and colourful thoughts. It's also about emptying it of chatter.

brilliant tip

Whenever I get creatively 'stuck' it's because the stimuli that get my juices flowing aren't in front of me. So I try to fill my mind with stuff that makes me laugh or gasp, or which thrills me. I look at colours. I smell the roses. To achieve creativity I need to be thinking about flowerbeds not spreadsheets.

Step seven: Getting hot ideas flowing

Pouring cold water on any idea is very easy. What is needed is a way of getting those around you to feel comfortable in trying to be creative. Create a creative environment linguistically by using positive language.

Negative body language and 'yes but-ism' can destroy genius. I think that's why Van Gogh cut off his ear. He'd just finished 'Sunflowers' and someone came in and said 'Hmm. Hmm!! I don't know. Do you think people like dahlias?' So write a list of positive words and try to embed them in the way you think and speak when you are in a group creative session and see how things change. This is not so much for you, who should be beginning to get the sense of how to unlock your creative potential, but for the others who will be transformed by your positive responses.

Here's a menu of phrases that get people to relax and generate ideas:

- Why not?
- Let's build on that ...
- Yes ... yes!!
- When can you start?
- I'm a mean-spirited bastard but even I can see something in that...
- 'Imagine how much work it must have taken to make it look this easy' is how Nike decribed the way basketball players LeBron James and Kobe Bryant played in the Olympics. Watch them talk and play on YouTube to see how true this is.
- Let's try this out ...
- I'm not sure but prove me wrong – go on – I dare you
- Yes ... a big yes
- Yes ... a small yes ... but a big hope and even bigger support
- Go on
- Love it
- I'm thinking ... OK ... yes let's do it
- Can we put that one in the excellent pen?
- I'm speechless ... with praise
- Approved. Excellent. Next ...
- Hands up those who think this is a crap idea – no one? OK. Approved.
- Thank you, well done, amazing ...

brilliant timesaver

The reason creativity often takes so long to get flowing is because we aren't thinking positively. The quickest way to change that is to start talking in an upbeat way. Find colourful positive language that motivates people.

Step eight: Get ready to be creative

Well how? I've already talked about the power of questions. The key is to get everyone around you to get into questioning mode because this will jump-start the process of creative thinking. Imagine you are about to go to a creative workshop or one of those meetings where a team is supposed to solve an intractable problem.

If you could write a few words on a card to get you through the day these would be the big ten questions:

- What?
- Why?
- How?
- Where?
- When?
- How much?
- Why not?
- What if?
- Where next?
- What next?

The reasons they jump-start the brain is that they force you to seek the problem and define it, not simply guess at the answer. Ask those questions and you will create a robust fact-defined brief. They are also incredibly useful next time someone asks you to make up a story.

Step nine: A creative exploration

This idea is very simple. You need to practise it an hour at a time.

Write down the brief in one sentence.

'We want to launch Brand X with maximum noise and minimum cost in four weeks' time.'

You can ask these questions:

- What is the product and what does it deliver?
- How big is the market?
- Who are numbers one and two?
- How big are numbers one and two?
- Who are the people most likely to buy this product?
- Where will the product probably be distributed?
- How much profit is Brand X targeted to generate in years 1, 2, 3?
- What is the price of the product?
- What is the quality of the product compared with numbers one and two?
- What is your overall reputation with your customers and likely consumers?
- How important is this brand to us?

Here's a moment of maximum creativity. This is a 'creative game'. So you can answer the questions yourself and then try to figure out as many ideas as you can to achieve the launch successfully.

Here is the really useful part of the exercise for this or any other real exercise you do. When you have generated a lot of ideas, divide them into

- weeds – they aren't very good – throw them away;
- flowers – they are pretty but are they useful? You can eat nasturtiums, for instance;
- vegetables – things that are good to eat and will keep you alive.

Create a concept of the 'creative greenhouse' and put the vegetables and the best flowers in there so you can 'bring them on.'

The gardening analogy may be helpful as it's full of useful metaphors:

- thinning out
- watering
- applying Miracle-Gro
- getting rid of bugs and blight
- transplanting.

You will have got the idea.

You've got yourself into the frame of mind that is going to get you and your colleagues (if they've followed the same process) ready for a big group workshop. This is a step-by-step process and you need to respect the mental gymnastic process involved, but already you have given yourself and your co-creative-spirits the best chance of making a 'creative workshop' work. Better than that, you have begun to attune yourself to stretching and expanding *your own mind*.

Creative thinking in business comes from thinking in a relaxed, curious and dispassionate way. In business we are not about creating masterpieces so much as things that really work and add value, profit, market share and productivity.

Step ten: The big 'hallo'

Virtually everyone has to introduce themselves at meetings or workshops. They usually do it rather badly and apologetically:

> Hi, I'm Richard. I work in Procurement which is, well, quite interesting and I want to see how today goes really ... and I suppose that's about it really.

That's more usual than you might think. We are awful at saying 'hallo – I'm me'.

Practise so you have an introduction that has impact and is witty and creative.

> The chairs you're sitting on, the light bulbs above our heads, the daffodil bulbs in the gardens. Mine. Prised from suppliers. I'm called count-your-fingers-when-you've-shaken-my-hand. I'm a Buyer. I'm in procurement. My name is Richard. And today I'm buying into that stuff called creativity.

Hopefully you will get the idea from this of (as they say nowadays) 'giving it some' or being 'well introduced'.

Step by step you've got there. You're on a springboard. The real excitement begins now, you've had your warm-up. Creative thinking is something that doesn't any longer feel alien, so now it's time to get to work with your peers.

brilliant tip

This isn't a competition – it's a collaboration. So make sure you are nice and encouraging to all your colleagues. It will work so much better if you do that.

🔁 **brilliant** recap

- Everyone I work with is always chuffed to find how creative they actually are.

- Creative in business means being different, not being Einstein.

- Try seeing things from a different point of view.

- Imagine that you got to exactly where you wanted and then work out the four or so steps that let this happen.

CHAPTER 7

A creative checklist about you

I n this chapter I invite you to take stock of where you've got to in this process.

You've done warm-up exercises and you will have thought a lot about creativity; about whether you are strongly creative, potentially creative or not very creative at all; about whether you've ever been creative or whether your innate creativity has been educated out of you.

There are also some creative stimulation techniques to help you get ready for working in larger groups or in 'creative workshops'. But first of all, some truths about creativity and teamwork.

Creativity: the essential tool

Creativity is essential in business if the people in it are going to be adept at change. Change is an unavoidable characteristic of the world today so we all need to be capable of doing it, but to do it well we need to be smart and creative. By being creative we'll introduce change in the imaginative kind of way that enables it to be bought in to by everyone.

> change is an unavoidable characteristic of the world

Creativity keeps you fresh

When you read a new book or listen to new music you are embarking on a creative adventure. The human brain is hard-wired to embrace innovation. That's what drove Columbus or Vasco da Gama or what drives playwright Tom Stoppard or any leader of any business.

You were creative once, even if not now

Virtually all children are creative. They play. They make up stories. They inhabit rich worlds of make-believe. They create new games with their own sets of rules. They draw, paint and think in primary colours. We were all like that once. So what happened? Appalling leaden-footed teaching submerged our creativity and turned us into competent process engineers, great project managers but apparently devoid of ideas. 'Apparently' is the key word because our task is to 'un-suppress' your latent and original creativity and get you dancing again, intellectually and imaginatively.

Why teams matter

I take the importance of teams in business as a given. But perhaps it isn't that obvious. Working in groups nearly always produces better, more effective and more imaginative solutions than anyone working on their own can produce, but a lot of talented people like working on their own. Importantly the reality for them is that in teams you will always have challenge, pushback and people asking 'what if?' That is why teams are inevitably the best way of

> working in groups nearly always produces better, more effective and more imaginative solutions

generating lots of ideas that could be made to work. Teams seldom produce ideas that are totally off-brief or impractical.

brilliant timesaver

Teams that work well together will always find a better answer but more importantly much faster than someone working alone. Good teams have their players playing to their strengths. That speeds things up.

Are you ready to roll?

If despite your efforts and my advice the light bulb moment hasn't yet happened, don't worry. Here is a checklist to help find out why and do something about it.

All are marked on a five-point scale where 1 = strongly disagree and 5 = strongly agree. And please don't be modest.

- Do you think you are creative?
- Do you think you are less creative than you used to be?
- Do you think you could be more creative?
- Do you think your colleagues are more creative than you?
- Are you more creative working in teams than on your own?
- Is your working environment helpful to creativity?
- Are you expected to be creative at work?
- Are you a fast thinker?
- Do you enjoy going to new places or trying new things?
- Would you like to be more creative?

Most exercises of this kind will produce – across the board – similar results with most respondents scoring around 30. But there are really three key barometer questions here: numbers 3,

9 and 10. And if you haven't scored more than 10 and hopefully more than 12 on those I'd be surprised.

Wanting to be more creative, believing you could do it and being curious about innovation are the keys to achieving your goal.

Creating the perfect conditions for you to think creatively

Here are some more questions which help you be clear about the circumstances which give you the best chance of being creative.

- When's your best time of day, morning or evening? Are you a lark or an owl?
- Where do you feel most relaxed when working? Think about where you feel most productive.
- Do you prefer thinking on a PC, a laptop or on an A4 or A2 pad?
- Do you want silence or background music? If the latter, what?
- Do you have enough light? Research shows we perform much better in bright light.
- Do you want it warmer or cooler?
- What's the ideal mood for you to be in?
- Do you want your room tidy or untidy? A large number of people I've spoken to go on a tidying up frenzy before they start work. Others like unstructured chaos.

⊿ brilliant do's and don'ts

Always make sure you are prepared to embark on a creative adventure. Do behave like the pilot you'd want to fly with. Do not take-off before you've gone through your pre-creative flight check. Do not fly without radar. Do not fly having imbibed alcohol.

Allow ideas to simmer and stew

I have talked about dreaming as a way of achieving creativity. The other way is to ensure that the key ingredients of the issue you are trying to solve are given the space and time to stew in your brain without trying to come to any particular conclusion. Not coming to a conclusion is hard because we've been educated to look at an equation or a question and answer it before that invigilator says 'will you stop writing now?'

The process I'm describing lets the intuitive part of our brain take the issue and then, as it were, cook it. *I love the idea of stewing your ideas in the Aga of your mind.*

Remembering your good times recreates them

Recall an occasion when you had a lot of good thoughts. Recall the place and the situation. What was it that made this stand out? What was special? What was different?

When all else fails reboot your mind.

Remember when everything felt great for you and you came up effortlessly with great ideas. Just recalling that will help you reconnect with your creative inner self.

Self-confidence is infectious

Whenever you are asked to come up with some creative ideas there is a sequence of thinking that helps get you running on that creative treadmill.

- I can do this.
- I shall do it very well.
- I am in charge of my own destiny.

- I shall discard more ideas than I keep.
- This will be fun.

Creative exercises to ignite your imagination

These exercises allow you to flex your creative muscles and find out how to get the most out of your imagination. They involve discipline and question-asking as well as free-wheeling thinking. The time you spend on these in private will be very useful when you find yourself in a creative workshop or a team brainstorm. But remember to warm up first.

Imagine you were in total charge ... what then?

Imagine you'd just won a large sum of money and that you've bought the business in which you currently work. You have carte blanche to do what you want with it. It's your money; your choice; your business.

- Whom would you fire?
- Whom would you recruit?
- What products would you drop?
- Where would you locate Head Office?
- How would you change the marketing?
- Where would you reduce resources?
- Where would you increase resources?

- What would you expect the company to look like in three years?
- What other five things would you change?

The creative challenge is to be able to imagine being in this position of power and imagine the consequences of all the decisions you'd make. The power of creative thinking is that it allows you to see things from different points of view.

See it from a different point of view

Most of us have so much information in our brains that we're bursting to make connections. The trouble is we struggle to be fresh because our left brain is trying incredibly hard to put things back into boxes.

Release your imagination. Imagine you were you, a child, someone living in great poverty, someone with huge wealth, someone from Saharan Africa, someone from China.

Try drawing each of these as though you are the imagined people above (and don't worry about the quality of drawing – it's the idea that matters):

- house
- dog
- plate of food
- family
- an office
- man at work
- woman at work
- countryside
- city.

The lesson will be that you will have to think about ideas from different perspectives: 'People only see what they are prepared to see' (Ralph Waldo Emerson); 'What we see depends mainly on what we are looking for'(Sir John Lubbock, scientist).

Organising your ability to recall connections

'Mind mapping' is a powerful way of creating order out of chaos and teasing out the vast body of knowledge, perception of patterns and connections motivated people can generate. The technique proves how much we know when we create the right structures even if we didn't know that we knew them before we started.

🡵 brilliant exercise

How many types of tree, uses of trees, fruit from trees, etc. can you come up with, in half an hour without and with mind mapping?

How it works is you assemble a list of subheadings under the word 'Trees'.

- evergreens
- deciduous
- fruit
- used for furniture
- foreign
- diseases of trees
- people who deal with trees.

The lesson is that we can make more connections and be more creative if we are organised.

Generating ideas when a group can't get together

'Brain-writing' is the same concept as 'brainstorming' but done in writing around a group of people like the game 'Consequences'. Half-formed ideas are built on and passed on and passed on. This works especially well with a group of smart people trying to crack a very hard problem.

What's so powerful about this is that those people who through nerves or wanting to avoid looking pushy have a technique here designed to work with that critical thing, a team, in building a group-built idea. It works best with smaller groups of three or four. It also works well with just two.

When you feel in a manic panic

Everyone does. A sense of un-control. The sense that everything you most need has been lost. This is not the mood you can be in if you want to have some interesting new ideas.

Try 'mind dumping' which is 'brainstorming' without the rules. Spend half an hour simply writing down all the things that come into your head. It will prove as therapeutic to get rid of a lot of mental rubbish as it is to tidy your desk. And you may, while you are doing it, discover a thought or two that's useful or that you'd forgotten about and had rolled into the corner of your mind.

The best way of helping solve a problem

Now that's a big claim but when you have to advise someone or give yourself advice there are three things that matter:

- the advisor is on your side (empathy);
- the advisor has been in a similar situation (identification);
- the advisor has had a solution that worked (resolution).

I think this concept is brilliantly creative. Chris Dugdale (a magician like Nick Fitzberbert) has reduced this three-part creative solution to most problems in a simple script. It goes as follows:

I know how you feel about ... I felt the same way when ... but I found that when I did ... everything worked out just fine.

Are you ready?

If you're not sure then I have this to say to you:

> I know how you feel about creativity and in particular creative workshops. I felt the same way when I went on my first. I felt nervous but more than that I was worried about making a fool of myself. But then I met this guy called Richard Hall who talked to me about the subject, gave me some techniques to practice which I did. And everything worked out just fine.

↗ brilliant recap

- This is pre-flight check time. Are you ready, are you qualified and do you want to be creative?
- Everyone is much more creative than they think.
- Improve your chances of doing well by working in environments that suit you best.
- Practise exercises which build creative muscles.
- Remember yourself as you were at your best and try to be like that again.

CHAPTER 8

Creative crunch time: 'team techniques' for creative workshops

The menu of techniques shown here all work but you need to choose the right technique for the right situation. There are three typical situations:

- A business problem or group of problems that need sorting. (Example: The factory in Lille is way below other factories in the group in terms of productivity.)

- A big strategic issue. (Example: Where is this business going? Where could it go? What does it take to get it there?)

- Innovation. (Example: There's a need to create a raft of new products to refresh the current product portfolio.)

Clearly the last option requires more freewheeling energy than the other two.

brilliant tip

We are all more creative than we think. The techniques that I've described are the equivalent of creative WD40. Try them and use them to loosen yourselves and become idea generators. Astonish yourselves and have fun.

Learning to be creative is like swimming

When you do get into creative workshops, the chances are you'll be surprised that not only can you swim but that you can also do butterfly, crawl and backstroke.

the more you do, the
better you'll get

The more you do, the better you'll get and the more you do, the more you'll want to do.

This chapter is the handbook to the techniques that make workshops fly and there are enough here to enable you to make the first few workshops all quite different.

Health warning: Do not try creative exercises without doing warm-ups first

The warm-ups are not nice-to-haves. They are essential. We are dealing with complex and precious equipment here – your brain. Treat it with respect.

Secondly, most of what you'll do is re-learn what is second nature to a 7-year-old.

Creative workshops, when done well, are enormously productive and even better fun.

Take your time. Be patient. Start the engine. And when you are ready, put your foot down …

Why run a workshop?

This is the most important question you can ask. If you don't have a clear set of objectives or better still just one or two things to fix you oughtn't to be running a workshop. Be clear with all your delegates before they arrive as to what the aim of the day is.

Who will be in it?

Do not try to run a productive day with more than six or seven people. When you have a roomful of 12 or more you are a hostage to mob rule.

There is of course a solution if you have to have 12 people involved, which is to run two workshops. It's strange that some people don't seem to think the numbers matter. They do. With six or seven you can create and control momentum.

Do not invite anyone who is a dyed-in-the-wool cynic or has no real need to be there or any contribution to make.

↗ brilliant do's and don'ts

What impairs creativity is protecting your piece of corporate turf and being personal (It's my idea that matters; What's in it for me? Am I looking good?). So don't do that.

Do share, listen, encourage and try to build something.

Where do you run it?

Try to run it off-site with all mobiles turned off or better still left at the office. For preference, try to find somewhere interesting with a decent view. Try to avoid windowless or underground rooms. If the budget stretches to it, stay overnight. This secures a fast start in the morning provided people don't stay up very late drinking too much. If it has to be in the office make sure the room is dressed up a little so it looks as though the person organising this 'event' cares.

What's it like?

Remember the word 'Event'. If the day is really going to be a success make sure it's memorable.

brilliant definition

The perfect workshop. 'It was a completely memorable day full of ideas, laughter and fierce debate. I learned a lot and we made huge progress in solving what felt like an intractable problem. A brilliant and inspiring experience'. .

The following four things really count in having a workshop that participants will judge a success:

- Good facilitation or chairing of the event. The motive is to keep everything moving at a good, businesslike pace.
- A decent, brief record of the day. Brief is harder than expansive by the way.
- A clear and thorough briefing on what is going to happen. If you have seven hours available try to break the day into, say, no more than ten segments. Make sure there is enough time at the end to drive towards a conclusion.
- Branding and art direction of the room and all the material used stick in people's minds and the event is given a particular focus and importance because of them.

One technique which always kicks off well is the 40-second self-introduction designed to be creative (see Chapter 6 but remember it has to feel fairly comfortable for you or, at any rate, natural for you).

Things you can do in a workshop to make it swing

The acid test of a workshop is what you and your fellow delegates get out of it, not what you put into it. But there are a series of techniques and 'games' which help groups give of their best and forget their inhibitions.

- You have got to start the day with everyone on the same page and 'warmed up'. If the people there aren't ready to go for it and get stuck in, the chances are you are going to have a pretty unproductive day. So make sure everyone arrives ready. Try to get broad alignment but don't aim for blind obedience.

- You should only expect to use at most three techniques, bearing in mind these are tools to help everyone maximise their creative thinking. None of them is magical; all of them are pragmatic ways of helping people think more adventurously.

- The rules of engagement are:
  - There must be no invalidation of ideas – no negative pushback.
  - We need a lot of ideas not just a few good ones.
  - Big, colourful and off-the-wall ideas can be helpful.
  - We need to build on ideas and see how to improve them.
  - Everyone is equal; this is not a hierarchical game.

Ways of getting groups to start thinking creatively

Brainstorming

Brainstorming is the most common technique and one that depends on a dynamic and highly encouraging facilitator for success. Alex Osborn, an advertising man, created the idea of brainstorming in 1941, claiming that the technique increased idea generation by 44 per cent (which sounds suspiciously like ad man statistics). It is quite simply a free-thinking, generative process where nothing is taken for granted and where the association and connection of ideas is encouraged.

How does it work? By getting people to lose their inhibitions and say what they are thinking, which is then gathered, developed and passed on by the facilitator and developed and challenged and developed and passed on....

Remember no one owns an idea in a brainstorm.

⤷ brilliant do's and don'ts

Do make these sessions move at great speed with lots of encouragement to participants. Do learn to lose your reserve, do say what you feel and think. Don't try to own an idea as your own. Don't be competitive – this is about teamwork.

Finding new ways of looking at things in a disciplined way

Edward de Bono's concept of *lateral thinking* is out on its own in this environment of getting a group to develop interesting ideas. This is 'brainstorming' done at a rather more gentlemanly and sophisticated canter. It has a real sense of structure as you can see.

- First of all set up the task, the objectives and the background.

- Constantly break up the way of working and thinking so no one settles into a rut.

- Imagine you could have anything you wanted to solve this problem – what would it be?

- Think opposites – what's the opposite of what you have?

- Think similarities – what is this like?
- Make people challenge facts – must it always be like this?
- Encourage people to change the rules.

<blockquote>encourage people to change the rules</blockquote>

- What if? Why not? Encourage different thoughts. Encourage creativity.
- Write stuff down so ideas get captured – A2 pads – lots of magic marker colours.
- *Legibility matters.* A good scribe matters.
- Stick the sheets on the walls with Blu-Tack.
- In general three hours of intensive open debate is about as much as any group can endure.

Getting people doing verbal cartwheels

The use of the 'word association' game is often productive and mind loosening and which sometimes produces rich content as people get in the swing of it. It works best when done in sequence going round a group. If you can't think of a word say 'pass'. It's interesting to do this at the beginning and then again at the end of a session to prove how dramatically everyone's improved.

Example:

> Loss – funeral – closure – recuperation – renewal – birth – growth – city – noise – excitement – bars – people – laughter – opportunity – friends – sharing – shares – sell – cash-in – re-invest …

In itself this will produce no worthwhile ideas but it can warm up a group who are tired or one that needs waking up. If you want to make it competitive to up the ante, do so.

Teaching people to squeeze the juice out of a story

Get people in a group to develop the most powerful sales story they can possibly find and deliver for any product you care to give them. In doing this you help them see things from various points of view and use their imaginations. In one of my groups a potato was compellingly sold as a multi-purpose device. I've never been other than astonished by how inventive people can be. The power of detail is important in helping develop an idea but not just detail, detail which translates into human benefits. Doug Hall (no relation) in his book *Jump Start Your Business Brain* develops the sales argument for Armor Shoe Polish engagingly thus:

Basic feature	Human benefit
Fast shoeshine	2 minute shine
Durable shine	7 day shine
Protects shoes	Salt guard vs winter damage
For all shoes	Gentle shine for delicate shoes
Whole shoe care	Special anti-slip for soles

The ability to describe a situation or a product in the kind of detail that involves and excites people can be transformational in helping create a really exciting workshop especially in the generation of new product ideas.

How do you get a group grounded, animated and inspired?

A brilliant way of starting a 'workshop' is to split the group into two teams and send them for a long walk down a high street and through a shopping centre the afternoon before the creative day or on the morning of the day itself. Ask them to take pictures of stuff that interests them so on the day itself they can identify and debate ten big trends in retail or society that is going to inform their view of the future. The big story could be anything or anyone from a *Big Issue* salesman playing the fool, a child stroking a cat, an overflowing litterbin or a new branch of WH Smith. The first trick is to be on the look-out for the unusual. The second trick is to relax in each other's company. The third is to give yourselves time.

brilliant timesaver

The time you spend creatively solving problems together saves time later on. Really difficult, company-threatening challenges deserve time and energy in their solution. *You can never be too busy to discuss how to survive (or better, to thrive).*

Putting life and colour into the way we see things

We live in a technicolour world but we are, most of us, using monochrome minds. It's the nature of 'work' today that means we lose our sense of virtually everything except survival.

This game involves our using pastels – messy but easier to clean than paint – working as a team and constructing a mural on lots of A2 sheets pinned together of a subject like 'The High Street of the Future', 'The Office of the Future', 'The Seaside of the Future', 'The Motorway of the Future'.

It helps to have a semi-professional artist on site to draw the outlines under instruction. The participants' role is to colour in what the artist has given them. Colour speaks. Try it. This requires lots of boldness and expressiveness.

Life is visual but business is about reports: change this in your meeting

If it is true that 'a picture is worth a thousand words' then we should spend more time building our corporate picture libraries. Whenever you see a good picture – one that describes what you do or feel – capture it, because thinking visually and not just in documents is an intensely liberating experience.

In a group session an hour spent going through twenty magazines each will be a stimulating exercise in creating the beginning of a library and proof of how hard it is to find useful and inspiring images.

We need to use all our senses – touch, taste, smell, hearing, sight: I am suspicious of mood-boards which are at best very approximate things and often totally misleading. Whenever I see them I am convinced how very good art directors in advertising are.

A 'mood room', however, which touches every sense is a great place in which to hold a 'workshop' about a business issue that needs resolving. It's also going to take a lot of collective thought to get right. It needs six people (including a chairperson) with each of the others representing a separate sense. How for instance would you create the mood room for the UK government?

	Primary	Secondary
Touch	Lots of paper	Leather chairs
Smell	Dust and whisky	Hot (as in air)
Sight	Suit and braces	Empty green benches
Taste	School food	Claret with lots of tannin
Sound	Sheep baah-ing	Non-stop 'order, order!'

Or you might see it very differently. Just try it for your given topic and see what happens. The point is to try to extract the essence of the experience by focusing individually on each experience because it forces you to think really hard about what makes a brand, a company or a specific service experience special.

Seeing things from different angles so you learn something new

I just love this technique and think everyone should use it daily. Ask a group of people to debate the opposite of what they want, for instance, 'how could we sell a lot less than we currently do?', 'how could we worsen our customer satisfaction?' or 'what small change would make our product worse?'

In the answers small but very telling truths can emerge like 'do more of what we currently do – that should make things worse'. This might force everyone to examine whether the seeds for the brand's destruction don't already exist. GE created an exercise during the dot.com boom called 'Destroyyourowncompany.com'.

brilliant tip

Reversal is about 'flipping' so you see things from a completely different perspective. The Unilever Chairman who said to his ice cream executive 'never mention the weather' forced them to stop thinking of hot and cold and to start thinking of ice cream desserts.

Change the lens through which people look at things

By distorting dimension so the issue you are dealing with appears as either much smaller or much larger you change the way people think about things. Example:

- Suppose the problem we are talking about existed only in one town like Bath – how would we address it?
- Suppose this was a global problem and getting worse. How would we deal with this commercial pandemic?
- Suppose this was the only problem you had … what would you do?

Teaching people to take nothing at face value

I heard this one (more or less in this form) from ex-advertising guru Len Weinreich.

There are seven glasses of clear liquid in front of you. Examine the different ways you respond to each as I tell you they are:

● tap water

● bleach

● pure spring water from Ochran Mill in the Wye Valley

● sulphuric acid

● saki

● vodka

● distilled water.

Playing the game like this in which nothing is quite as it seems is a potent way of creating new product concepts, hence Croft Original which looked sophisticatedly pale but had the sweet hit of Harvey's Bristol Cream. It also lies at the root of much of the new-wave cooking at El Bulli or the Fat Duck.

It reminds us to never take anything at face value.

Thinking hats revised and reinvented

Edward de Bono created six thinking hats:

● **White** – about information

● **Red** – about emotions and feelings

● **Black** – about caution, criticism and challenge

● **Yellow** – about optimism and positive thoughts

● **Green** – about creativity and opportunities

● **Blue** – about seeing things from above – deep thought.

Too many hats? Too many to be really useful in a workshop. Let's reduce it to three, says Nick Fitzherbert, and let's use T-shirts, say I:

- **Red** – do we think it's a good idea?
- **Yellow** – why's it a good idea?
- **Black** – what could go wrong?

The T-shirt wearers are the arbiters of a days' work. From their different perspectives they can sort out the weaknesses and strengths of different ideas. This can provide a pretty sophisticated sieving process.

Sorting out good ideas and learning not to lose potential brilliance

Research, according to de Bono, has shown that when people are asked to sort ideas into 'Good, Bad and Interesting' that usually the most useful ideas (or half-formed ideas or ideas that might lead to other ideas) sit in the 'interesting' category.

Try this yourself at the end of a workshop so the half-formed 'interesting' gems aren't lost. This is because interesting can lead to new places; good has already got there.

Learn how to tell stories

brilliant tip

Once upon a time in a wild and adversarial workshop the facilitator picked up a paperweight and ... Learning how to create and tell stories is a great way of getting to understand a business problem.

↗ brilliant recap

- Before you do anything else in planning a workshop be very clear about why it is being held.

- Be careful you recruit the right number of people – six or seven is an ideal number.

- Go for a bit of 'wow' factor, but if it has to be on-site dress the room to make it special.

- Rules: no invalidation by anyone; everyone is equal; everyone contributes; we go for lots of ideas.

- A skilled facilitator makes all the difference.

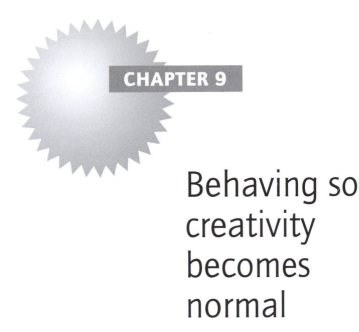

CHAPTER 9

Behaving so creativity becomes normal

T his chapter encourages everyone to learn how to embed creativity into their organisation and into their own performance. It's about helping develop creative minds that are dependably and consistently effective.

Embedding creativity into our places of work and making it normal involves getting buy-in from a lot of people (especially from HR), and then it means living the belief. Every part of your business has to believe 'we are creative'.

Creativity isn't an occasionally worn coat – it's closer to your skin than that. In fact it's an attitude you never take off. Learn how to root it, feed it and grow it and learn on a personal level never to forget the Gary Player mantra: 'The more I practise the better I get.'

Making the most of creativity

If you have a skill, use it. Razia Iqbal of *The Times,* in writing about the National Campaign for the Arts, reflected: 'The most important identifying characteristic of the UK is creativity.' Meanwhile Lord Puttnam says that we, in Britain, have 'some weird genius for coming up with good ideas'.

Is Britain good at creativity? Look at our advertising, our arts and, when we can get the money, our films. And look at some of our great brands – like Branston and Hovis.

While other parts of the world are doing amazingly creative things now the British are innately inventive and are great at teaching creativity. If we can do that then we can, also, relearn the skills that originally gave us our creative reputation.

Become a creativity champion

What is needed is a group of people throughout a big business, especially if it's multinational, who are coached in the finer arts of running workshops, who are themselves really good at creative thinking but more importantly are noisy advocates of it and stuff that's going on in the field. These are the eyes and ears on how to manage the process and constantly improve it.

Whether you are a manager, merely a hard worker or running your own business, in order to make creativity normal, someone needs to grab it and champion it. Volunteer to become a 'creativity champion'.

Have a statement of what you stand for and make it a good one

Mission statements puzzle many people because so many are gratuitously self-serving, banal and impossible to apply. Here's one that is typical in spirit (although blessedly short – it's only merit):

> To achieve excellence.
> To respect my colleagues.
> To go that extra mile.
> To leave my desk tidy.

This one from Goethe, is both stirring and rich in aspiration:

> Whatever you can do or dream, begin it.
> Boldness has genius, magic and power in it.
> Begin it now.

And this, from Interbrand, the marketing and branding giant, is really interesting and gets nearer to what I have in mind than most do:

> Each day
> We start a new life.
> We are seekers of possibilities
> Finders of new ideas
> In unlikely places.
> We know we can change the world
> Because
> We can change
> The way we see the world.
> Think of the things
> We can do
> We can
> Because we believe,
> We can,
> So do.

I particularly like the idea of finding new ideas in unlikely places.

People who want to be creative are creative

A.G. Laffley of P&G and the Saatchis both brought to their respective organisations a love of outsmarting competition and a mood of creativity that was all-pervasive. Greg Dyke seemed to do this briefly at the BBC as did Tony Blair with New Labour. Steven Spielberg does it wherever he goes.

The real key – in a larger company – is getting young and ambitious people, especially those in HR, to buy into the idea of creative thinking and recruit people into helping who conform to this ideal. There is little point in talking about creative thinking while your HR peers are off recruiting left-brain process-engineers.

creativity does not belong
at the top of a company;
it has to be everywhere

If people hear that creativity is at the top of selection criteria in recruiting new people, word will get around. Creativity does not belong at the top of a company; it has to be everywhere. And it needs to be well signposted.

The key creative signposts

In any office building you can signal what you stand for in the following places:

- **Car park**. Is yours a horribly hierarchical place with visitors parked somewhere at the back and titles or names of directors stencilled on the tarmac?

- **Reception**. Is yours clean, tidy and busy? Are guests greeted as though you are really glad and interested to see them? Is it in touch with the real world, showing breaking news on TV? Are there interesting things to do with the company you can look at? Does it feel creative?

- **Meeting rooms**. Most meeting rooms are boring rooms, not places where ideas happen. What's on the walls? Second-rate paintings – very bad; a white board – good; a montage of stuff relevant to this particular meeting – even better. Creativity is helped more than anything else by visible evidence that people care about its existence.

- **Canteen/restaurant**. The Google canteen in their Zurich HQ says more about the care and creativity of Google than anything else. An abundance of Ben & Jerry, fruit and Lindt chocolate also equals abundance of ideas. Is yours a happy lively place with animated conversation or is it dour and uncreative?

- **Corridors**. Don't stack boxes in your corridors, fill them with coffee machines, put pictures of your products on the wall or put up notice boards about health and safety and company procedures. This is where you live. Is it exciting? Is there any evidence of creative thinking or of humanity?

- **On the phone**. Does the person who answers your phone sound switched on and enthusiastic? Alert, alive, interested and prepared to have a conversation? The key word is alert.

- **Website**. Have a look at the Innocent, Warburtons or Ben & Jerry websites – all terrific. A website is a brilliant place to proclaim: 'This is who we are and what we stand for. This is what we want to achieve. This is what we think being good means. And if you like what you see we'd like to talk to you.' If you want to embed creativity in your business do *not* have an uncreative website.

- **E-mail**. Your emails say a lot about you – individually and collectively – in the way they look, how they are signed off and broadly their tone of voice. Persuade your colleagues to do themselves and your business justice by creating emails that are cheerful, interesting, short and clear.

- **Meetings**. The way meetings are set up, especially workshops, will say whether you are creative or not.

The way you run or plan a creative workshop says what you stand for

You have embraced the need to be more creative and to learn and use the techniques that will get you there. Now you need to help set up your own company's workshops in a distinctive way. You and people like you can have a big influence on the way things happen if you can prove you are really keen to help.

> you and people like you can have a big influence on the way things happen

There are various levels of creative coaching:

● **Introductory** – a short course, probably less than a full day. It will have maximum fun and participation. This is a useful way of filtering out people who might have exceptional creative potential.

● **Intermediate** – something like a two-day course, tackling some major challenges in the company on the first afternoon and second day.

● **Advanced** – a three- or four-day programme, one part of which should involve meeting a group of customers, people who actually buy the products or services the company sells (the only rule here is that the customers need to outnumber the delegates by four or five to one). The point of this exercise is to allow the people on the programme to really get to know the sort of people who use and who sometimes grumble about their products.

Tools of creativity

There are a few ways of making a workshop more impactful.

● **Creativity in motion.** Have portions of the day filmed and then cut into a two- or three-minute clip with music so every member who goes on a programme has a permanent record of the event inspired them.

● **Branded items.** You need everything you can brand to reflect what you are trying to achieve – pencils, pads, mugs, T-shirts, agendas, stress balls, tissues, bags, books and so on. Make the day belong to creativity.

● **Making people really want to go to them.** Build momentum, run a series of programmes and do them so well you'll be besieged to run more programmes. Once word gets around that they are fun as well as being effective they will become a magnet for more ideas.

▶ brilliant example

Insights into the story of Honda. I met Martin Moll who is the UK Marketing Director of Honda. Their creativity really stands out. Try this from a Honda fan online about one of their commercials for the Honda Accord which comprised a complex domino sequence of car parts falling one after the other. It's amazing: 'Everything you see really happened in real time exactly as you see it. The film took 606 takes. On the first 605 takes, something, usually very minor, didn't work. They would then have to set the whole thing up again. The crew spent weeks shooting night and day ... It is fast becoming the most downloaded advertisement in Internet history.' Creativity is the DNA. Here's what a former President said: 'We sometimes experience an unexpected breakthrough when we begin development without theories and try various things while not being afraid of making mistakes' (Kiyoshi Kawashima, President 1973–83).

Creative techniques that become second nature

Have the curiosity and confidence to focus on half a dozen of the techniques described and practise them. Practise them until they become second nature.

Which half dozen do you choose?

Choose the ones that suit *you* and which you most enjoy. Mine are as follows:

- **The long walk** – window shopping and people watching. Trying to work out what is going on out there in the real world.
- **Mind mapping** – this is a brilliant way of unearthing all those things in the grey to dark, half-forgotten area of your memory.
- **Reversal** – doing what would achieve the exact opposite of what you want can sometimes expose exactly what it is you are now doing that is wrong.

- **Thinking backwards** – allows you to define and actually picture success and plot how it was you got there step by step. It's a kind of 'pre-rationalisation' and one of the most creative tools there is.

- **The stimuli binge** – sit down with a pile of books, papers, magazines, spend an hour surfing the net, listen to Radio Four, spend a couple of hours flicking through the different TV channels. And they call this work!

- **Positive language** – as we get tired of, and (it's the word of today) a little *stressed*, our language begins to get more negative and lacking in colour. Try writing a couple of pieces brimming with lively words and excitement. Learn the rhythm of positive language.

brilliant do's and don'ts

Don't be lazy. Learning to think creatively is just as difficult as playing music. No one who wanted to be any good at either would dream of not practising. Do be rigorous about practising specific techniques until you get really good at them.

brilliant recap

- Be part of a cadre of creative followers in your business. Eyes, ears and voices.

- Get the support of HR and top management. Creativity is never nourished without top level support.

- Check out you deliver positive creative signals at all your key customer 'signposts'.

- Create highly branded 'creative workshops' that are distinctive, popular and effective.

- Make your own creativity dependably repeatable by practising your own favourite techniques.

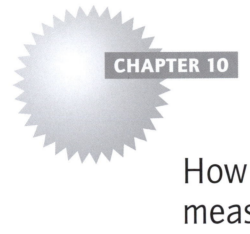

CHAPTER 10

How to measure creativity

The precise world of work

Business today is intensely driven by data and the need to measure things. This sometimes means the ability to sell a creative solution is going to be hard, especially when a rational, numbers-focused, left-brained audience is eyeing the creative solution with suspicion and is sceptical that it will produce an adequate ROI (return on investment).

Many believe if you can't measure something, it has no value. Examples of things hard to measure are morale, potential and creativity. As Warren Buffett said, 'I don't measure my life by the money I've made. Other people might, but I certainly don't' (cited in *Warren Buffett Speaks* by Janet Lowe).

Learning how to live in this world of measurement

In a world of key performance indicators (KPIs) measurement is regarded as essential. We want to measure children at schools; we want to measure climate change; we want to measure crime rates. Measurement can tell us where we are and where we've come from but it can't tell us where we are going. There's an old aphorism which is anti-excess measurement: 'If it swims on water and it quacks, it's a duck.'

brilliant tip

We need to validate hypotheses so don't take anything at face value but if the evidence for something is overwhelming, move on. You don't need to keep on measuring the same thing – time is money.

Measurement dominates fast-moving consumer goods. At one time RHM, who owned all the major salt brands (Cerebos, Saxa, Sifta and Stag), took Nielsen (the retail research study) at considerable expense to track brand shares in salt – not really worthwhile.

The trouble is measuring things can be an obstacle to changing them. We need to measure things but we also need to do something more old-fashioned called 'gauging'.

The lost art of 'gauging'

Learning how to better gauge situations is a major aid to creativity because it involves taking an overview of a situation – assessing broadly the scale of a situation. And creativity thrives on broad rather than precise micro-measurement.

creativity thrives on broad rather than precise micro-measurement

Gauging was very important in times prior to the existence of useful scales and tape measures when traders had to gauge by eye and by feel the weight and volume of item A versus item B when they were bartering. Now gauging is a great way of applying practical measurement and assessing whether something is working. Gauges on machinery, for instance, tell you if all is well or if some point of danger has been reached.

Get skilled at working out how things are going. Get skilled at doing exercises like this – how many people are there in a hall, by judgement, not by counting? How heavy is something? How long is something? What's the temperature?

People who become overly reliant of a calculator become poorer at doing calculations in their head and become in thrall to the accuracy of the machine even when it stops working properly – 12×30 = 3400 – well, unless your gauging brain is in action with a 'hang on, that's wrong', you are in trouble.

Gauging with numbers works the same way as the instinctive brain 'knows' when something has been spelt erroneously.

↗ brilliant do's and don'ts

Do develop your instinctive feel for what's right and wrong. Don't underestimate the calculator in your head. Don't close off your memory bank by assuming the computer knows best. Do recognise you are much cleverer than a computer.

Gauging creativity

Creativity is hard to measure except in the results it produces, but I'm going to try because we need to pin down the way a creative idea has its own individual impact on a group of people trying to solve a problem. We've said we want to avoid allowing a hyper-critical atmosphere to exist because this stifles creativity. However, we have to at some stage allow ourselves a way of grading the impact and influence ideas have. Try the following six-point scale of creativity:

● **Er?** An idea that does something but at first seems a little confusing … maybe something to be built on.

● **Oh!** A moment of real impact but maybe not quite what you'd expected.

- **Hmm!** That's an expression of appreciation – a 'well, that's very interesting' moment.

- **Ah!** A definite breakthrough. The mind is beginning to fizz. We have a definite moment of insight.

- **Aha!** The authentic 'now I get it' moment. This is when the temperature in a room changes.

- **Wow!** Likely that a room will split between 'wow!' and 'er?'. Wow moments come infrequently and are when a great leap has been made. But beware – not everyone will get it. Wow! was when the wheel was invented.

brilliant timesaver

If you can create a league table of creativity which acknowledges there are differences between good and excellent, between 'nice idea' and 'we've got to do that now!', then you will have managed to make creativity seem a much more important business tool. Best of all you will have saved a lot of time debating how creative an idea is.

The smell of creativity

Malcolm Gladwell in *Blink* writes in praise of the accuracy of intuition, especially in experts. Art aficionados will often spot a forgery instinctively because alarm bells go off in their heads. A long period of rational analysis may actually persuade them they were wrong (our educational system is very powerfully left-brain oriented) when their first instincts were right.

It's that 'gas moment'. If you smell gas, you call British Gas, you don't wonder if you might have made a mistake.

The smell of creativity in a company starts in the reception of a business and the first steps into a building. The first impressions, the tone the people running the business are happy to give, the way they are happy to say 'welcome – this is us'.

Three examples.

Dunlop

It was the 1980s and nearing the end of its existence as a UK business. All was not well at what was called Fort Dunlop, a vast complex adjoining the M6 at Birmingham. It smelt of British manufacturing industry at that time; slightly unwashed and very unfit. Reception was drab and dirty but what was astounding were the corridors with a succession of expensive and closed wooden doors that characterised the place, a bit like the Woolworth HQ of the 1970s. *Imagine if business life was a succession of closed doors. It used to be, but not any more.*

August Storck

This is a huge German confectioner that's privately owned. They also own the Bendicks brand, Werther's Original, Merci chocolates and Toffifee. Their sugar confectionery plant is in Halle, just north of Dusseldorf. It's very rural. The factory when completed was surrounded by trees planted to hide it. There are meadows left to grow naturally, a butterfly park and a lake where the staff swim. Going in their reception is like walking into a friend's kitchen: 'Hi, you must be Richard.' Needless to say it's very creative and brilliantly run.

Years ago the general manager Otto Panke was running a meeting and suddenly cried out, 'What's wrong with everyone? Why are you being so uncreative. I'll sort this. Everyone take your clothes off'. It's one way, I suppose.

A man called Marsh

Allen, Brady and Marsh was an advertising agency which in 1979 was the fastest growing in the UK, winning several major accounts. Peter Marsh was a populist and a showman. He clearly agreed with the point about receptions. They pitched for the British Rail account ('it's the age of the train', 'let the train take the strain', remember them?). When the board of British Rail arrived at the agency they walked into a filthy reception, ashtrays overflowing with cigarette stubs, newspapers on the floor, stained settees, old coffee cups and a blousy receptionist on the phone to a girlfriend. After several minutes of this they got up in rage about to leave when Peter walked in wearing his characteristic white suit saying something like this: 'Gentlemen, this is how many people see British Rail. It's not good. Follow me and we'll show you how you can change it.'

Creativity can dramatise things and change perception. You can smell the aroma of creativity.

When measurement stops and faith begins

The design company The Partners cited research in June 2009 which showed when it came to creativity in business, 96 per cent of companies agree it's integral to success, although 40 per cent say no one is responsible for it yet and only 10 per cent talk about it at board meetings. The irony is in the exactness of the measurement and the absence of creativity's presence.

creativity is essential

Creativity is essential and you don't need to persuade the most enlightened about this, but equally there is no accurate or telling way of applying measurement to it.

There's an act of faith here, plus some rudimentary tools I've described. But perhaps the most telling thing you can do is create a benchmark in the business in which you work.

Ask them

Create a simple questionnaire for your company (say a cross-section of 10–20 per cent of the total workforce with these questions. All to be marked on a five-point scale (5 = very, 1 = not at all):

- How creative a company would you say each of the following is:
  - Apple
  - Google
  - Nike
  - Sony
- How creative would you say the business sector in which you compete is?
- How creative would you say your company is?
- How big a difference would it make to your company if you were more creative?

The results you get from this may be the only formal bit of measuring you have to do to make creative thinking a 'must-have' not a 'nice-to-have' in your business.

If you can say 'the industry benchmark is a 3.2 and we only scored a 2.4' you will capture a lot more attention – measurement is embedded in businesses so use it to your advantage when you are selling the importance of creativity.

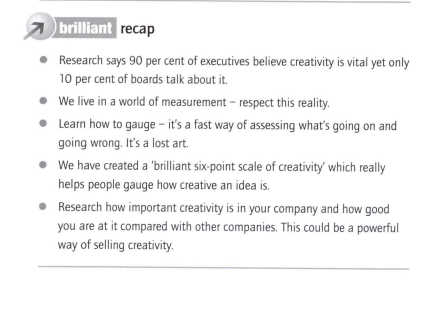

brilliant recap

- Research says 90 per cent of executives believe creativity is vital yet only 10 per cent of boards talk about it.

- We live in a world of measurement – respect this reality.

- Learn how to gauge – it's a fast way of assessing what's going on and going wrong. It's a lost art.

- We have created a 'brilliant six-point scale of creativity' which really helps people gauge how creative an idea is.

- Research how important creativity is in your company and how good you are at it compared with other companies. This could be a powerful way of selling creativity.

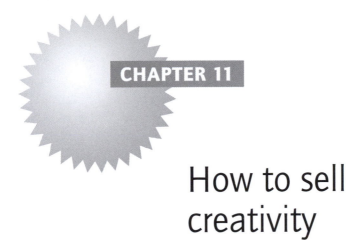

CHAPTER 11

How to sell creativity

The world of persuasion and the useful tool called numbers

The key jobs in business are management of systems, management of people, management of money and management of sales. If you can't sell stuff you can't survive. But to return to data, it is always smart to have numbers in your sales pitch. Those who don't always respond well to creativity always respond well to numbers.

> if you can't sell stuff you can't survive

A guide to selling creative solutions

There are some basic principles that you need to adopt in selling a 'creative solution':

- **That it meets the brief** that you had been given. Spend time simply analysing and expanding on the brief and answering the question that needs answering. Now is the time to prove you are a serious player and not a dilettante.

- **That this was teamwork**. If it was work done by you on your own make sure you refer to everyone you talked to in coming to your proposal. Show there is no ego involved here. Teamwork beats solo work because it means a group of people believe in the task.

- **Being heard is vital.** Because we live in a crowded and cacophonous world we need what creativity brings to a solution: a greater likelihood of its being heard and seen and thereby a greater capability of gaining traction. Creative ideas attract attention.

Contextualise the problem that needs to be solved

Whatever it is you are working on put it into context. You can't be creative in a vacuum.

- How does it have impact within the company?
- What is the background history to the issue?
- How does this relate to the wider world?
- How have others dealt with similar problems?

you can't be creative in a vacuum

- What current circumstances influence the way in which you will approach the issue?

brilliant tip

If the issue has been about downsizing, how have other companies dealt with this and what have they learned from the experience? People from other companies are usually happy to be very open and helpful about their own experiences. A creative solution is only any good if it works. The downside of a cleverly creative solution may have been seen by others who can help you avoid getting into unnecessary trouble.

Koestler, that extraordinary polymath, talked about the imperative of effective implementation of a creative idea. Rightly, because a badly executed 'good' idea is probably worse than a brilliantly executed weak idea.

Understanding the ramifications and the context of an issue can help you avoid a bad piece of execution or a bad piece of selling. Like the story of the poor bear.

brilliant case study

The story of a bear and a wood

This happened a long time ago when advertising was beginning to come so powerfully into its own as a creative force in the United Kingdom. The proposed commercial was set beside a log cabin in a pine forest with a presenter talking to camera about the benefits of wonderful, pine-smelling Airwick Solid as an air freshener. In the background but unseen by the presenter a ' bear' creeps up darting behind trees, crawling through undergrowth, absorbed clearly by the presenter's words and reacting to them. The client said 'what's with that bear?' and out of hand, rejected the commercial as silly.

The bear was, of course, a comic bear whose antics acted as the punctuation and counterpoint to an otherwise very straight piece of advertising. The bear was 'us' – asking all the questions we'd ask as consumers: Is it true? Why's he going on so long (yawn)? Is this stuff really any good? (Big nod of approval from the bear.) Yet, all the client saw was gratuitous creativity. Or maybe we sold it really badly; our fault, I guess. The key fault in selling or in failing to sell is in failing to put a creative idea into context and framing it properly. Selling has its own logic and it needs to be understood and applied.

How to sell a creative idea

Identify the problem

State very clearly the problem that needs to be solved or the opportunity that needs exploiting. Use facts and figures to show you have a very clear understanding of the scale and scope of the issue.

Dramatise the problem

Problems have an impact on a number of things, but take just four to start with. You need to find 'colourful' stories or evidence to dramatise each:

- people
- sales
- profit
- reputation.

Show you empathise with the respective effects that problems bring to each.

Problems are not always explained by a logical piece of paper, they are the gremlins that walk the corridors of every business in the world. So, to achieve the colourful effect I am recommending, try to find an anecdote which explains the true ramifications of the problem you are seeking to solve.

find an anecdote which explains the true ramifications of the problem

Describe what getting rid of the problem will feel like

Show what it feels like with (and without) the problem:

- when that gremlin is alive (and is kicking)
- when that gremlin is dead (and, happily, buried).

You should be seeking to infer (like a doctor might) what it will really feel like being well again.

Outline the logic of the solution

Before you show the solution, describe the logic it must fulfil and the implications that will flow from it. This is very much left-brain stuff but it's important the audience hears a controlled, rational being selling to them, and not a creative maverick who has no regard for life after the solution.

Establishing your credentials and the fact you are obsessed about numbers, implementation and accountability (as well as ideas) is really important.

Present the solution, showing how it fits that logic

Be very clear that the solution logically answers the brief. Explain it so an audience can see this as a logical choice and one that having creative edge will gain traction that much quicker. Remember as a general rule that 'creative' thinking leads to more cost-effective results.

Show how the solution tests or a similar solution has worked elsewhere

It's helpful to describe how something broadly similar has worked out. The effort of getting the wisdom of other people in other companies looks professional and gives reassurance.

As a rule saying 'this has never been done before' does not inspire confidence whereas 'something similar was done at x – it worked but in retrospect they think it would have worked better had they done z' is helpful learning.

Avoid being precious

Although you want to win your argument and do a good sales job, do not get precious and 'sniffy' if it doesn't go your way.

You want to be seen as a logical as well as an inspiring presenter but you can only be as good as you can be. If you rehearse enough and have the argument well worked out all should be well but there are no guarantees in life.

brilliant tip

In selling, prepare carefully, do presentations with controlled passion and respond to reactions from your audience, but if you lose the argument be gracious, find out why and learn from it. Do not blame anyone.

Lifting the odds in your favour

In Japan the meeting is there for show. All the serious stuff's been done beforehand.

The really smart thing to do is to consult with everyone who's going to be at the meeting and try to pre-sell them.

Although this takes a lot of time you'll end up with a greater certainty of achieving what you want.

brilliant timesaver

Pre-sell to as many people as you can so the basic sales job has been done before the formal presentation. You'll find this saves a lot of time.

Understand that the person you are selling to is a messenger. Remember that everyone you present to will almost certainly talk to other people about what you've said. Better still, give them a one page acetate crib sheet (acetate because it can't be torn up or easily damaged); one page because we live in busy times and people have low boredom thresholds.

The use of drama in selling

I've talked about being a little dramatic mainly because drama is a way of making what you say more interesting and the story more engaging. I am not recommending you should become extravagantly theatrical but do give your pitch a little life and passion. I mean, you do believe in it, don't you?

The best salesman I ever saw was Tim Bell (now Lord Bell) who brilliantly empathised with his audience and made the whole creative process seem natural and fun. He seemed like a very smart coster-monger who would play poker with you, taking your money but leaving you feeling like a winner. Selling is about telling a story. So be a great storyteller. Make sure what you say is very clear and well understood. Ensure the people you are selling to get the story firmly in their heads.

Always end up talking numbers

Creativity is a means to an end and that end is solving a problem but solving it in a clever, cost-effective and inspiring way. Solving a problem involves a cost and a return on that investment. Creatively solving it should produce a better ROI (return on investment). Creativity and numbers need to go hand in hand. *Always be very specific about what this return will be. In the end business is business. Remember that the ability to measure things and sell solutions go hand in hand.*

Life is full of unexpected happenings

Seth Godin (writer, speaker and self-described agent of change) said: 'Starting a new company, going on sales calls, inventing a new product is all about scenario planning. The fun is figuring out a back-up for whatever could go wrong'.

Anyone who's spent any time selling anything knows that disaster lies round the corner. You try to sell an advertisement about a joke cat to a client whose cat which she idolised has just died. The answer is to be highly attentive, responsive and creative.

↗ brilliant recap

- For many people in business numbers are like music. Use numbers to sell.
- Sell logically and methodically. Be dispassionate.
- Creativity frightens some, so don't be flashy.
- Put the creative solution into context and try to find real-life analogous situations which inform the solution you have.
- Try to pre-sell to the people who matter. It saves time and conflict.

CHAPTER 12

Using our creative minds to design change

The single most important asset that thinking creatively produces is the ability to explore the unknown and to juggle various hypotheses. Given the contradictions, complexities and unknown territory we enter in the modern world it's an asset that's useful to have.

What I've created here are simple examples of scenario planning that executives looking at long-range strategy should be accomplished at working with. The two specific creative exercises relate to the 'lives we live' and our 'world of work'. The invitation is to read the brief and the prompts given to speculate as to how each might develop and what levers you can push to change things. In short, what are the practical changes you might make to 'debug' the present and create a better future?

The most creative work you can do is to try to imagine a better situation than you are in and then work out how to get there, using timesaving and creative techniques we'll describe as we move on.

brilliant timesaver

Always split a problem up into smaller components. Example: Solving the problem of running London may paralyse you but if you split the problem into functions and then geographical areas and so on, it seems a bit easier.

Time for inspiration

You have to take time out occasionally to look around at what the very best do and have done and speculate how on earth they got to do it. What drove them? What spark ignited their imagination?

So let's briefly reflect on the top ten inventions in shaping today's society chosen by the Science Museum:

- 1712: the Newcomen engine. The first practicable steam engine which pumped water from deep coal mines. It demonstrated the energy source that was to drive the Industrial Revolution.

- 1829: Stephenson's *Rocket*. The first credible steam locomotive.

- 1837: the electric telegraph. It predated the Morse system and was used to catch a murderer travelling from the scene of his crime in Slough to Paddington.

- 1896: the first X-ray machine. Amazingly invented by a schoolboy, Russell Reynolds, and his father.

- 1908: the Model T Ford. The mass-market car that foreshadowed and powered the revolution in the way factories worked.

- 1928: penicillin. Fleming's discovery was the single biggest breakthrough in treating infectious diseases and saved millions of lives.

- 1944: V2 rocket engine. Wernher von Braun's nasty weapon teed up the technology that made space travel possible.

- 1950: Pilot ACE computer. The Automatic Computing Engine was the precursor to the modern PC.

- 1953: model of the DNA spiral molecule. Watson and Crick transformed our understanding of the human body by discovering the double helix structure of DNA; the way that life works.

- 1969: the Apollo 10 command module. Used in rehearsing the moon landing of later that year.

Visitors to the museum are invited to create their own order of importance for these inventions so they have the final say in ranking.

So what's missing?

Well a couple of biggies like the water closet invented by Sir Thomas Harrington in 1596 but in Victorian times popularised by Thomas Crapper (no, I'm not joking) and the World Wide Web created by Tim Berners-Lee (1989) might have expected to have made it, as might aspirin (1889), beta blockers (1960) or the phonograph (1877).

There will be disagreement about what constitutes the most important innovation (the one that has a beneficial effect on the most number of people); the most creative innovation (the one that makes the biggest leap); the most life improving (the one were we not to have we'd regret most). We need to be clear about the rules before we make our list.

But making such lists as this, given we have a brief, is a profoundly creative exercise in itself because it involves making choices.

An exercise in mind-stretching

This exercise shows how in an hour or so we can stroll through some of our day-to-day life (excluding work), see what's changed and think hard about the kind of changes that might happen next.

It's better to attempt this as a group than in isolation, but have a go anyway if you're on your own because although your ideas

the key is to ponder about what is and what might be

may lack group dynamism and momentum, you'll be driving forward, exercising your creative muscles. The key is to ponder about what is and what might be.

You'll find it easier to do this under a series of headings: fifteen are given below with some questions or 'prompts' under each.

You are starting to become a really accomplished creative thinker when you can paint speculative pictures of the future that are credible and interesting and which help inform your strategic thinking. The trick is to be free-flowing and imagine the impossible or unlikely. If you struggle *divide your thoughts into three categories* – what you'd really *like* to happen, what you *fear* might happen (worst case scenario) and what you *think* might happen.

Creative exercise one: 'how we live'

This is not a complete list but a useful starting point from which to generate new, interesting, helpful or even mad ideas. How about this from the Netherlands? Houses without foundations which float if in floods – and that's true. Brilliant.

How about dividing a house into cooking-eating, playing-relaxing, studying, wash-relaxing and sleeping units where the sleep-component units are small, efficient places rather than the space-wasters we currently have?

Now it's your turn. Remember you don't have to be a genius, just curious, observant and relaxed. On seeking to be really creative and original remember what the one-time US President Woodrow Wilson said: 'Originality is simply a fresh pair of eyes.'

- **Every room in your house** – how would you change it? What matters most? Imagine your favourite home-of-the-future – what's the most important place?

- **Your garden** – what's it really for? – the extra/outside room – garden toys – garden offices – sustainable gardens – low maintenance garden – children's garden – the garden you eat – garden parties – gardens that are redecorated – seasonal gardens … and so on.

- **Children** – what they need, do, eat, play with, learn, where they go. What games do they like? When and how do they need family? What does 'alone' mean? How could it be done better? What's for better or worse? How do we make them happier?

- **The street** – street furniture, transport systems, lighting … what are streets for? Walking, driving, parking, cycling, trams, what? Police patrols, graffiti, street corners …

- **The local community** – self-sufficiency – allotments to feed the neighbourhood, the 'Big Lunch' (that's the recent community project organised throughout the United Kingdom getting local neighbours to get together in parks, green spaces and have a jolly good lunch together), street parties, helping neighbours, getting back to 'village' mentality.

- **The facilities** – school, church, playing fields, libraries, Citizen Advice Bureau, playgrounds, police, emergency services, sheltered accommodation – how do they work? What do we need? How to organise? Who decides what and how?

- **Travelling** – what are the forms of transport we most want to develop and how (walking, public transport, bike, car, motorbike, plane? – how should they be developed? – what kinds of car (the car of the future – commuting cars, pleasure cars, travelling cars?) – commuting, integrated transport systems?

- **Trips** – travelling abroad. Business – what's needed? Pleasure – what's wanted? Airports?! – luggage (what to do when/if no luggage allowed?) – size of planes – stations – trains – coaches – holidays. Adventure vs Sun vs Culture vs Themed breaks. Issues of comfort vs cost.

- **Social life** – pubs, gastropubs, clubs, restaurants, fast food chains, coffee bars, theatres, cinemas, gigs, sports, dancing, skiing, climbing, sports on, in and underneath water, extreme sports.

- **Foreign countries** – where's 'hot', where's going to be 'hot'? What are the creative ways that would make Britain (or your country of choice) become a greater attraction? (For a cautionary tale read *Au Revoir to All That: The Rise and Fall of French Cuisine* by Michael Steinberger).

- **Health** – How do you feel? Top to toe? What's changed? What were your mum and dad like at your age? Are you frightened by SARS, MRSA, swine flu, BSE, AIDS? What are the great discoveries that transform health? What's next? Are you worried or confident about the future in health? What would change your outlook?

- **Education** – what were the skills way back, in post-war years, in the 1980s and now? What's the good stuff, creative-breakthrough stuff and not such good stuff? What's made schools and universities better places ... think facilities, technology, more tests, more course work/fewer exams, more choice, sex, drugs and rock and roll? What's changed? What sort of people shall we need in 2050 to run the world? We shall start educating them in two years. Do we know what we are doing?

- **Social services** – All the things that government does for us from paying benefits to collecting rubbish to arresting people to parking fines to all the work the NHS does to the way mothers and the elderly are treated. What signs of success should we look for and what are the key issues? Some say we are paying benefits to the wrong people. Others say we are storing up problems by failing to solve the problems of creating an impoverished underclass.

- **Government** – does it work? How's it changed? What has got better? Think of the number of departments, the changes in accountability, the antiquity of Westminster, changes in technology, think select committees, think media power/influence, think electorate power/or lack of.

- **Green issues** – what's got greener and by how much? What 'new' green ideas can we see? What's improving? Where are the world breakthroughs? How are companies responding? Who are the good and the not so good guys? Why does it matter? Has world recession put 'green' down the agenda? What do our children think about this? List the bugs which you think we need to address.

Pause for breath (and an apology)

When I, and others like me, run creative groups we seldom expose people to exercises as comprehensively as this at an early stage. But the reality is that the gallop through the world in which we live and asking questions on top of questions on top of questions (see above) brings out all those latent bits of creativity that hard work, reading too many papers and not having enough time has suppressed.

If you've gone through this and it has provoked in you, as it surely must have done, a cavalcade of new thoughts then I am very happy.

Creative exercise two: 'how we work'

I've taken the starter prompts a stage further and am challenging you to take a more radical view about how to make your place of work more congenial, more stimulating and more productive.

We are talking about jobs which, for many of us are, to be blunt, more about being seen to go through the paces than go an 'extra mile' or make a 'creative input'.

We want (nearly all of us – and certainly any half-decent CEO wants it badly – to change that). So we are talking about building those conditions that aid creativity. Now that most of us busy people have showers rather than baths the opportunity to stay in soft focus and think creatively has reduced even further.

---

brilliant example

Here's how Teresa spends her week. She's in marketing with a large global company, married but without children. She plays tennis and goes to the theatre when she can. She has a long commute by car and once a week flies to the continent for meetings, staying there overnight. She is regarded as a high flier; her husband who's an investment banker says she looks knackered.

She spends 39 per cent of her week working; 25 per cent asleep; 12 per cent travelling; 16 per cent having fun; 8 per cent eating.

She's 30 years old. And she's worried that in her last appraisal she got a low score for creative thinking. When asked how much time she spent on it she reckoned she crammed in a 'rushed' two hours a week. Her cat spends more time than that on working out more elaborate tortures for the mouse.

	Hours per week	%
Work	53	32
Working at home/hotel	12	7
Commuting	12	7
Work travel	8	5
Relaxing	17	10
Recreation	5	3
Entertainment	5	3
Eating	14	8
Sleeping	42	25

In this context working out how to improve Teresa's life and creative output is rather important. By spending a day a week at home, doing a day's work in just 5 hours, she'd gain 8 hours (including the gain from not commuting) to spend doing and thinking creatively. This must be the way to go.

Manage your life so you stay sharp and always have enough time to think clearly and creatively.

Your challenge is to question everything at work. Use the suggestions below to spark off some interesting ideas.

your challenge is to question everything at work

Head office/branch office

I know one business that has so many offices no one knows where anyone is. I know another one where the MD has banned home working as he doesn't trust his staff ('they'll just watch TV all day').

But why do we need offices? What is all this crucial work we need to do in a building? How about a trophy office which people just use for meetings and for important get-togethers and creative workshops? How about an office in an extraordinary setting – overlooking the sea or a great view?

Your office is a cost. Ask what it gives you. Ask whether it's needed. Question the cost.

Open plan

When they introduced open plan in the 1970s at Beechams (as it then was, on the Great West Road) everyone brought in plants which grew rapidly. The smell of jungle was stifling and demonstrated that people want to be separated from colleagues.

Open plan beats offices but you need to make it work, not just impose it on people.

How about open-air offices in the summer? How about themed offices reflecting current initiatives? In something called the 'Washington Experiment' researchers discovered that any changes in the workplace increased productivity. So paint the offices red, then green, then blue. Open plan is great if it looks good. Who wants to work in an untidy garage?

Standards of offices are poor. So try to raise the game. Work with your colleagues to make yours a 'proud-to-be-working-there' place – then creative thinking and a sense of shared endeavour will flow. And if someone says that's 'unrealistic' tell them they lack ambition.

What are your ideas on these?

Hot-desking

Google regard this as a repellent and soul-destroying practice which proves that a business hates the individual. And there's some truth in this because up to now it's just been done badly.

How do you do it so it looks as though you care? Mood desks, for example – quiet desks, creative desks, team desks, budget desks, solution desks and so on.

So how about 'cockpit-desks'? Work stations which like a 747 cockpit have everything you want within 180°– the cockpit surrounds you, providing a soundproofed environment. You have three computer screens and one of those you can turn into a mood-changing scene of a golf course or a busy city or a jungle. Your Nespresso machine is inbuilt. So too are headphones for your phone and iPod – big squashy ones like pilots use. To make the thing more fun you could create new buttons for the computer to enable you to see KPIs dramatically shown on a dashboard of dials (Sales Barometer, Staff Turnover, Customer Satisfaction ratings, Performance vs Budget and so on). Create this as an exciting working world.

Don't underestimate the value of toys. Work should be fun too. What are your ideas for creating relevant and well-branded fun?

Break-out/meeting rooms

Make them interesting. Why do offices have to be so dull? Give them relevant names but don't take it too seriously. Names like the Sales Drive Salon; Strategic Review Control Room; The Numbers Room; Off the Wall Gymnasium; New Product Kitchen.

Naff? No. Not done well and thought through. This is a way of creating impact and potential excitement. Creating excitement is a key tool in motivating people.

What would make a difference to the productivity where you work? What do you need to focus on?

Off-sites

Have fewer off-sites in more interesting places. Use the War Rooms in London or see if you can do something at one of the palaces in Britain. Go to the Eden Centre and have your meeting after that, or have it on a naval boat at Portsmouth. Have it in a hospitality suite at a major football ground or Twickenham or the Oval. Do it at the top of Tower Bridge. Or go somewhere that symbolises what you want to tell people: Land's End – we are in deep trouble; a flight over Everest – to emphasise that this is how high we need to go; a ride on the worst fairground ride ever – Space Mountain might do it – to say we have a journey to go and it might be a rocky ride.

Do not be boring in choosing an off-site.

Acid test: will your delegates tell other people where they are going or where they've been in a 'bet you wish you worked for us' way?

Working from home

Do it once or twice a month at least. The discipline is to be quiet and remote. If you have a reasonably big garden, create a garden office (in effect a nicely painted and well-kitted-out shed).

Use the time to do things you wouldn't normally do – like going shopping, reading reports and books you haven't had time to previously read. And dress down.

Make working from home the most productive and creative day you ever have. Then they'll beg you to do it more often.

Virtual offices

These are commonplace through operations like Regus. You don't need to have an office or a PA to have people think you are ensconced in a plush Mayfair office – as if that really mattered. To some it does, so check this out so you can spend even more days working from home or out on the road meeting customers and getting a better feel for the marketplace.

Check you spend enough time with people who spend money with you. How could you give them more time?

Lunch

Do not be too busy for lunch or coffee or any opportunity you can find for meeting people. Lunch is not as Gecko in the film *Wall Street* put it – for wimps. Lunch is a great and cheering way of getting to know people. Breakfast and tea are also great ways of meeting in a different way.

If people make the world go round it's a good idea to make people happy and enjoy the experiences you share with them. Set up your own corporate monthly 'Breakfast Club'. See what happens. Get someone to talk for 20 minutes and then do a Q&A.

Over food, when they are feeling good, people will be less guarded and will often tell you things that make your job much easier.

So how could you be more entertaining – not more lavish – as a business?

Work clubs

New idea. Create places in cities to which corporations subscribe so their executives and executives from other companies can meet and feel they have a real and significant base. Think of it as Platinum Card Institute of Directors.

Think of stylish 'work clubs' as a compensation for getting rid of expensive head offices. Or are there better ideas like company gymnasiums?

The world of work as it changes

The way we work is changing but a vast number of companies carry on as though it were still the middle of the last century. Sandy Weill, when he ran Citigroup, had his own office in every major Citigroup office and in which a working fireplace was installed.

Another CEO worked in open-plan at Ogilvy chain smoking. Smoking was banned in the building except for him (the same used to apply to the Duke of Westminster – that lone puffer).

Old world	New world
HQ	My world
Private office	Sitting room
Status	Achievement
PA	On the move
Admin staff	Mobile communication
Routine	Reactive
Luncheon	Tea
Leaving late	Starting early
Meetings	Action meetings

↗ brilliant do's and don'ts

Do embrace the new 'creative' world – be a highly mobile, customer facing, internally coaching, confident spokesperson. Don't equate your status with your size of office. What did for John Thain, ex-CEO of Merrill Lynch, was the absurd amount he spent on his office. Carpet pile is not creative.

How big is my carpet?

The size of office used to say how senior you were, as did your carpet in the Civil Service, where someone I knew had nine inches cut off his carpet because the office he was given had too big a carpet for his grade. The day the size of office is seen as irrelevant will spell the dawning of a better working world. Stuart Rose has started the revolution at M&S – from the mahogany of Baker Street to the glass egalitarianism at Paddington Basin.

Maybe the CEO's office should be in reception where he or she can see and be seen. Imagine moving to a better place – where?

The place to be is at the heart of the business – not at the top of the building. It's only at the heart that creativity can be fired up.

PAs

What about the Miss Moneypennys of business? Consigned to history to be replaced by secretarial Asimovs (that's the humanoid computer invented by Honda). You'll be able to create its personality to match how you want to be seen by others. You delegate everything to the robot 'who' will sleeplessly be making sure you always look good.

How do you maximise your value and minimise your cost?

Coffee machines/canteens

Welcome the day when crazed executives attack the coffee machine and replace it with Nespresso quality. Also welcome the day when unhealthy sandwiches are replaced by high fibre delicious organic food that feeds people's brains. The sort of food they have at Google. Sushi, tapas, salads, smoothies, etc.

We shall see the institution of the lunch club revived with monthly 'lunchstorm'™ meetings. Lunches are occasions when people can share ideas, challenge, debate and have a free-thinking hour and a half.

What other idea-generating ideas can you come up with? Monday morning prayers; Friday evening sign off; monthly get-together?

Meetings

The time will come when meeting costs are metered. If the cost of having five national heads plus a limited retinue in a meeting costs at least £10 000 a day in salary alone, we have to ask if we are getting value. Is there a cheaper, faster better way of operating?

For many meetings are alternately 'the way we've always done it' or 'the true cut and thrust of political life in business'. *The reality is true creativity will be found in doing them differently. Smaller, shorter, more teleconferencing or videoconferencing. Big challenge – what are meetings for? Meet the challenge with shorter, better prepared events.*

Teleconferencing/videoconferencing

Teleconferencing requires greater skill than it is given. Trying to track who is who can be tricky and chairing the invisible is hard. Training in how to make the best of it will take place.

The quality of videoconferencing will dramatically improve using better lighting and much better filming. Videoconferencing will also be made a lot more interesting by having animation as opposed to video. A cartoon of yourself will create a much more interesting interaction.

There will be a drive towards making conferences more of a show with music, film and a real 'a sense of occasion'.

Be creative in making conferences dramatic. More ideas?

Whiteboards and interactive creativity

What you write on a whiteboard will be rewritten more legibly. Everyone in the room will have their own mini-board on which they can make suggestions which get transmitted to a 'master board'.

How else can you make 'brain-writing' work better?

PowerPoint

Presentations are the meat and drink of business not least because they force people to focus on their argument. PowerPoint is a fantastically useful tool for presenters, but very boring for audiences. The effect of bullet points is like being persistently jabbed in the chest: very irritating.

PowerPoint will reappear as a new, improved iteration 'PresentationPower'™. Presentations will cease to be an individual's responsibility and will be processed and improved by the communications people raising the standard and the consistency of output. Maverick, individual, last minute stuff won't happen any more. We'll see more film, animation, music.

Most presenters do it for themselves (the presenter) not you (the audience) – how do we change this?

The key to any big company – 'the need to impress' – will be fulfilled by the recognition that the quality and creativity of communications have to improve.

Inspiring creativity at work

We have got to change the comfortable old paradigm that work is about going to an office. So long as that and the old-fashioned 'command and control' model are in place, real creativity is going to find it hard to flourish. Go to the very limit of change. What would happen if:

- there were no offices
- the office was an enormous coffee lounge

- everything was open plan
- your HQ was an old Boeing 747 in the middle of an old airfield
- or an old control tower called (you got it) the Control Tower – which cocks a snoot at 'command and control' models?

Think the unthinkable; do the unusual; reach for the future.

think the unthinkable; do the unusual; reach for the future

This exercise will show you – if you do it with energy and conviction – just how many unusual, useful thoughts you can quickly come up with.

🔍 **brilliant** recap

- By splitting each situation or problem up into small components and walking our way through each part step by step, touching everything we do and questioning whether we could improve it, we shall find it easier to find a solution.

- Without descriptive detail we can't describe exactly what we'd change and how we'd change it.

- Relax. Think. Imagine a colder/hotter/drier/wetter world … imagine change and how we'd cope with that … imagine our ability to change things so we could achieve what we want.

- Most of all imagine a world where head offices, meeting rooms, mission statements, big offices and PAs are all history.

- Imagine working from your car. Imagine every employee being a salesperson. The Japanese already have.

- The twentieth century, old world is over. We are now global, flexible and unstable, in desperate need of the creativity that drives out been-there-done-that-doesn't-work-anymore thinking.

CHAPTER 13

Learning to play with ideas for profit

Scenario planning supports radical business strategies

Michael Porter said that scenario planning was where he really saw the value of creativity in forming strategy. He also touched on another key issue. You cannot solve problems or apply creativity in isolation to the context in which they exist.

A simple example of this would be in answering the question 'how do we increase sales?' because the question means two different things in a recession and in a growth market.

Speculating what the future might look like and illustrating it with specifics can be very stimulating and useful. Andrew Zolli (Z and Partners) said: 'To see the future, you have to look at this artful place where people come up with novelty all the time ... it is these highly imaginative individuals who reconfigure the landscape. You can't think about the future without having a playful mind.'

The future is going to be very different. We'd better be prepared for the likelihood of fundamental and seismic change.

be prepared for the likelihood of fundamental and seismic change

Fact is stranger than fiction

In 2006 who would have thought the following would have happened by 2009?

- **Economics** – The worst worldwide recession ever
- **World health** – A pandemic called swine flu
- **Sport** – A Briton breaks a world swimming record
- **Politics** – A black man becomes US President. Peter Mandelson becomes – however briefly – the most powerful man in UK politics.
- **Entertainment** – Philip Green and Simon Cowell go into partnership
- **Strange stories** – Sir Alan becomes Lord Sugar! Berlusconi, the Italian stallion!

Very few of the above could have been or were predicted. Even the previously impervious like Warren Buffett were badly burned. The real stories were stranger, much stranger even than fiction. It's time to learn how to envisage and paint a picture of unthinkable developments because doing so prepares one for the scale of change possible. To get the ideas which form this fictional scenario calls for a high level of creative imagination.

> learn how to envisage and paint a picture of unthinkable developments

⏎ brilliant do's and don'ts

Don't assume anything. Do expect it to be hotter, bigger, deeper or stronger than you'd have thought possible. Don't be conservative. We live in radical times.

Ideas are the currency of the future, ideas which change lives

The unthinkable is normal. If anything can happen we ourselves must be capable of creating the unthinkable to remain in charge.

Alanis Morissette, the Canadian-American singer-songwriter, expressed this beautifully in saying the following (and doesn't this capture the frustration so many of us have in the turmoil of today's workplace?): 'I want to walk through life rather than be dragged through it.'

You avoid being dragged through life by trying to conjecture the sort of things that might happen and plan how you'd cope with them and exploit them. This is where executives become explorers and exploiters at one and the same time.

A brilliant way of getting a group to exercise their creative muscles and learn the art of storytelling is by running a workshop on scenario planning. Here are some examples of questions to think about:

- It's 2020 ... what is the world like seen through the eyes of the man or woman in the street?
- Who's the US President?
- Who's in power in the United Kingdom?
- What are the leading cars, beers, restaurants, retailers, foods, fashions, types of music, holiday destinations etc?
- What's the weather like?
- What are the key items in the news?

The essence of scenario planning is to be provocative and to:

- make people think deeply about the future even if they disagree with each other about some of the conclusions – the debate and the recognition that if everything around one

is changing then one has to plan how to change oneself, will
lead to a lot of creative thinking

- strategise with greater precision

- question the long-term viability of everything

- realise that it's important that this isn't just an exercise in
fantasy – the more it is founded in facts and known trends,
the better.

More questions to stretch your minds

- Of the top 100 global companies, how many will exist in five
years' time?

- How will world economies behave? This may be a useful
quotation: 'Command economies fail because nobody has
the information needed' (James Whyte, *Bad Thoughts: A
Guide to Clear Thinking*).

*Our inability to comprehend precisely why economic turmoil happens as
it did in 2007/2008 will shape the way we behave in the future. Think
about how what has happened might shape our collective behaviour.*

- If the weather gets more extreme – hurricanes, floods,
extremes of hot and cold – how will this change the world
and business? What can we do? Who will benefit and who
will suffer most?

- What will follow swine flu? Are we about to see a massive
shrinkage of world population through serial pandemics?

- What will happen to the BRIC countries – Brazil, Russia,
India, China? What will happen to Africa? And how will Asia
overall fare – what of Indonesia which is slightly bigger than
the United States?

- Is the following creative scenario impossible and if possible
what would it mean for the world as a whole and the way
that business works? 'China has become the financial centre

of the world. If you are smart enough to be in finance you are likely to be smart enough to learn Mandarin pretty fast too. Shanghai is the most cosmopolitan city in the world. It is also now the city with the most Michelin star restaurants.'

- The big issues for companies could be the following – what else can you suggest?

  - Diversity – getting cross-cultural, cross-gender, cross-age, cross-ethnicity and cross-mood types to work together.
  - Environmentalism – packaging issues; general issues of pollution.
  - Talent development – what will be the most important factors? What role does creativity have in top talents' make-up?

- Local community development – local vs national vs global strategies.

In the tensions of the above what creative opportunities do you see and what are the most surprising changes that you think might happen?

- The arts – will they flourish or suffer? What arts will do best? Are Arts Festivals a thing of the future or past?
- How will education change – specifically the teaching of creative thinking and the sciences? What role will physical and sports education have?
- How about adult education?
- Will peace break out or will wars continue? Where is most at risk? What form will warfare in the future take?
- How will the world cope with ageing populations or will pandemics solve the problem naturally?
- How will politicians and people cope with food shortages? How serious a problem will this be?

Let rip ...

In scenario planning, the choice of a nightmare or a dream-scenario is ours. On balance the evidence points to a better future but with less wealth although a better quality of life. Strategising the future with some tangible speculations can be much easier.

Creative interpretation of the future isn't a sortie into fiction writing, it's the role of anyone at work. The questions asked above should get any group of executives thinking about the future in a vivid not a lacklustre don't-really-know way.

Here's an example of using creativity to imagine a consequence of the British financial sector becoming much less important.

⚡ brilliant exercise

'When Canary Wharf was closed down as a business venue to allow the creation of Blair Park with its phenomenal aviary and lakes it created a new opportunity', said Prime Minister Purnell, 'to relax and learn; adjust to a new world of curiosity, peacefulness and quality of life. To put Britain on a new map which looks to the future, not to the past and creating a future of inspiration not of economic desperation.'

Britain's biggest industry is Tourism followed by Demolition and, then, Creative Consultancies. Attracted by the climate and by the dramatic developments of Bournemouth, Brighton and Eastbourne (rebranded as BoMo, BriTo and EaBo) where most of the top companies are located – 'masses of graduates; universities doing leading-edge stuff in new technology; cooling sea breezes and big, blue horizons to help visionary thought,' says Lord Saatchi from Saatchi Towers (they call themselves 'The Ideas Engineers'). 'The park is built to resemble an enormous all glass liner sailing out of the Downs towards the English Channel on the site of the old girls' school Roedean to the east of Brighton.

In this admittedly racy piece of futurism there are a series of thoughts:

- That Tony Blair has become lionised in a big way – what happened?
- Labour is in power.
- That Britain has by implication moved down the economic pecking order with growth in wealth lower down the agenda.
- Tourism is huge in Britain.
- A lot of the old world would appear to have been demolished.
- Again by implication London is less important and new super-cities are emerging.
- Creativity has been put on a loftier pedestal than ever with the usual suspects in dominant roles.
- Might the demise of Roedean say something about the future of public schools?

I hope the point is made that once you start on such an exercise a raft of further thoughts emerge such as 'what would that mean?', 'why did that happen?' And if that happened it probably means ...

brilliant tip

Letting your imagination run riot, in time provokes you to think a lot more deeply and much more creatively about the future. Your own future, your company's future and maybe the company that you and colleagues should be forming in ten years' time.

We need to play more

Many of us have lost the knack of playing and it's losing that knack that makes us feel older and a bit more weary. Playing is not a flippant activity – it's the process whereby we get to liberate our thinking. Here's how Kevin Carroll, author of *The Red*

Rubber Ball at Work, put it: 'Play is serious business. It pulls ideas out of thin air, sees opportunities behind closed doors and creates solutions to your biggest challenges at work. Play puts the power of imagination, creativity and innovation in your hands.'

Scenario planning and creating stories about the future is a particularly powerful form of play. By stretching our imagination we can begin to see all kinds of possibilities that one would miss just being locked in the present. This is advanced creativity and it works because it should really make you think, debate and look for new things.

🡵 brilliant recap

- Michael Porter claims creative scenario planning helps create better strategy.
- You cannot think about the future meaningfully without having a playful mind.
- Fact is usually stranger than fiction.
- Create a scenario and then question and question again if it's radical enough.
- Have fun. Playing is a way of liberating your mind.

Conclusion: a world where your brain is still learning

What is creativity?

This is the really difficult question and, as we know, one which the *Oxford English Dictionary* conspicuously avoids. Creativity, the brief business definition, is the process whereby new ideas are produced. Remember that we are not talking about the creativity in art, poetry or the composition of music, which are much more intense in their demands.

Business creativity, the slightly longer version, appeared earlier in the book as follows:

> The ability to see new ways of doing things and a mindset which rejects conservative thinking. The process of idea generation which makes interesting connections. A restlessness to make new things happen. A belief that the status quo can always be improved and that our role in business is to change things so they become better/cheaper/faster.

This book argues for the need to practise creative techniques to aid creativity. All of us have hidden depths of creativity, not so much untapped as suppressed by years of ordinary, in-one-ear-out-the-other education. And if you accept this, that we are, most of us at heart, very creative, then we need to learn not so much how to be creative but to relearn how creative we really are.

A client said to me the other day: 'There's no such thing as a daft question.' Nor is there. The trouble we have is not asking enough questions. When a child enters the 'why?' phase of their life I'm pretty clear 50 per cent of the motivation is they perfectly well understand how tedious it is to be constantly asked 'why' but the other 50 per cent is because they have not been given good enough answers.

> Why is the world round? How do you know it's round? Is it slowing down? Does it feel funny at the poles because it moves slower there? Why are there so many stars? Why do people have wars? Why do people waste things? Why does it rain on my birthday?

creativity is about aiding understanding and change

The most creative way we can behave is to answer the hard questions in simple, accessible and engaging ways. And so, for me, the true art of creativity in the twenty-first century is simplification: the knack of making surprising but simple connections and creating metaphors that change the way people look at things. Because most of all, creativity is about aiding understanding and change. And it's about a continuing desire to learn.

Why creativity matters: the urgent urge

Creativity has suddenly become the hot topic in academic and business circles. Without creativity, we are told, the world will grind to a halt. What is required is creativity and provocation. A real sense of open-minded, 'anything is possible' debate. But the truth as we know is that business people are by nature exploiters and not explorers and that creativity is, in most businesses, a 'nice-to-have' not 'must-have' asset.

Yet we live in interesting, unpredictable and unexplored times. It's going to be difficult to exploit what you don't know about. And it's this – the 'I don't know what's really going on and driving us along any more' – feeling that initiates the urgent urge to innovate and change.

In the world today to recommend nothing should change is like telling a driver to ignore the brake and the steering wheel – 'we'll accelerate out of trouble' doesn't pass muster.

There is a basic human instinct and need. It's to innovate, refresh and repair.

The needs of business today

I suggested there were three key words in business today that dominate the current business landscape: *faster, cheaper, better*. There are two other words – *smarter* and *creative*.

The people in the *smarter and creative* school are the ones making waves. These are the people who are 'out-thinking' competition and who are 'repackaging' good ideas so they look like great 'creative' ideas.

We live in an increasingly better-educated world where the harder working Chinese, Indians, Indonesians, Brazilians (and they are very, very smart) are posing competitive threats and a deftness of strategic thinking we hadn't imagined likely. Not yet at any rate.

All our instincts in the western world are driven by a sense that we are effortlessly superior when it comes to creativity, hence the Italian opera, the Russian novel, the great German composers, French philosophy, Spanish art, British drama and poetry, the sheer chutzpah of American writing and of Hollywood. We need to believe we can still hack it and be exceptional creators of new ideas. (But beware phenomena like Bollywood in India – a creative and commercial powerhouse.)

We turned our back on the manufacturing sector for very good reasons (because others were better at it and cheaper) but that urge to learn and to tread on unexplored paths is still strong. And it needs to be. If we aren't creating, innovating and changing, we are lost. And if we aren't learning we are dying.

The profile of the complete executive

They (he or she) are all of the following:

- smart
- responsive
- curious
- hard working
- loyal
- very ambitious
- results focused
- agents of change
- clear thinking
- positive
- energetic
- productive
- diplomatic
- creative, creative, creative.

All the best people I've worked with are enthusiasts to the point of distinct mania, fizzing with ideas and seeming to move at a hundred miles an hour. Most of all they are creative. Because brilliant people are always creative and are always lifetime learners. They feed and flourish on the new, the unusual and on complex issues which call for supple and innovative brain-power to unravel.

brilliant people are always creative

Getting the brief right

It always sounds so utterly obvious: 'Plan your route before you start. Ask for directions if you get lost.' Getting the brief completely understood and agreed before you even twitch with creativity is vital.

The reason so much creative thinking has got a bad press in business is because it, too often, gets served up as a good idea in a vacuum not answering a specific need informed by definite constraints. This is where very direct questioning, interrogation – even an inquisition is required. Creativity in business which is not very precisely directed is like random bombing – impressive and frightening but not very effective. And an exercise that is likely to get you into all sorts of trouble.

Warm-ups, hot-spots and burn-outs

Your brain is an amazing piece of kit. It can outwit computers. It can create great works of literature or art. It can create amazing new products. It can make mistakes.

The fallibility of the brain is one of its most potent characteristics, because it is mistakes that increase our capacity to learn.

The phases of creativity are as follows.

- **Warm-ups.** There are a large number of different ways of getting yourself warmed-up. These could include solving a Sudoku puzzle, doing a crossword, doodling, walking along a high street or simply gazing out of the window with soft eyes. Warm-ups are designed to get you in the mood and it's in the mood you need to be if you are going to be creatively productive.

- **Hot-spots.** All of us know that moment when you are on a roll, when you get one idea after another, when you can tell a story with such good timing you manage to keep your audience in hysterics. But don't just remember that moment, try to recall precisely what factors led to your feeling and behaving in the way you did.

- **Burn-outs.** Do not underestimate the fact that creative thinking is very tiring. Anyone who's written a book will know this. Anyone who has run a series of workshops back to back will know what exhaustion is. You can get burnt out and, when you do relax, be kind to yourself, lie down, and when you feel a bit better do some gentle warm-ups. The trouble in business today is that the normal executive is unprepared to admit they feel knackered.

Creative workshops work

What most people in business need, on a fairly regular basis, is a quick pick-me-up. This is one of the functions of a creative workshop which serves a similar function in sport as a net, a quick kick-around or work on the practice range.

Creative workshops work at a series of levels:

- They help people learn useful ways of acquiring skills at finding connections between issues.
- They help people see things in new ways.
- They help people picture quite vividly how the future might play out.
- They help people roughened and glued up by the stresses of the day-to-day workplace get back on track.
- They act like WD40 – that magic lubricant which solves so many intractable probems.

Good, well-facilitated and energetic creative workshops are excellent places for people to develop their creative skills and relearn their innate talents at playing creative games.

Techniques that change the way you think

In business today the nature of workloads means a lot of people who are creatively talented feel unable to express this and just spend their lives doing project management (not that this doesn't need doing too). The problem is that there's an absence of innovation and creative thinking when all you're focused on is keeping the ship afloat.

To think creatively the following three key things are required:

- Time to reflect, time to explore and time to experiment. You don't make creative breakthroughs when you are struggling to keep up with your workload. Working out how to create the future deserves time.

- An environment and people within it who want to discover new stuff. The best breakthroughs and developments in business come with groups of people fuelled by similar ambitions working together.

- Most of all, people at the top of a business who can allow people to try things and fail. The importance of failure or the acceptance of failure is commended by thought leaders today. It's best expressed in the aphorism of Robin Cousins' skating coach in America: 'You've got to skate to fall.' Because it's only then that you learn how far you can go and how good you are.

Making creativity second nature

The answer is not to make it second nature but to reinstate it as normal. The wear and tear of busy lives spent looking at spreadsheets and attending constant meetings makes the art of creative thinking harder to practise than it should be and the creativity that most of us have – the storytellers we really are – gets suppressed.

The more time all of us can spend trying to work out how to find smart ways to be better at what we do, by working in groups, the more accomplished we'll get.

How to be recognised as a change master

Do you embrace or resist change?

Do you embrace or resist change? That's the key question. If you want everything to remain as it is you'd better think again because if that's your attitude you'll be very disappointed. Change is inevitable and it's happening now at apparently uncontrollable speeds. We do not live in a world that is in balance – economically, environmentally, medically, climatically or politically.

Are there reasons to be cheerful? I really think there are, but only if you are prepared to try and sharpen your creative wits and answer such basic questions as:

- How can we surf these waves of change?
- What new ideas have we got for updating our offering?
- How can we excite our existing customers even more?
- How can we attract new customers?
- What products or services could we invent that would catapult us ahead of our competitors?

Time is the constant problem

In a fast-moving, chaotic world, time is the biggest problem. Your most important challenge is getting the time, space and attention to think creatively, loosely, in an explorative way and stop saying you have:

- no time
- no resource
- no need
- other priorities
- a need to focus on the present
- to concentrate on the question – are we going to hit 'the number' this quarter?

Neither of the last two is wrong because business has to be managed. Spending time in a 'creative room' dreaming (however lucidly) will not necessarily produce the profit quickly enough to invest in the future if the red-alert priority is to stop the place dying through lack of sales.

The skill we must find is to find time collectively and individually to 'think'.

Lord Rutherford, the scientist, said: 'We have no money so we shall have to think.'

I am now going to misquote him: 'We shall have to think because we have so little time.'

Creativity placed on its proper pedestal

This book is about business creativity rather than artistic creativity. Business creativity is, by definition, a pretty pragmatic art, being able to create environments in which innovative ideas can emerge, developing ideas that have a great return on investment and, for you personally, to have the capacity and urge to have new ideas so as to advance your career. People who are acknowledged as creative thinkers are somewhat rare and regarded as valuable.

Change is what all of us must manage today. The smartest and the most nimble footed of us will do fine and enjoy the ride.

The key to whether we do well, exploit the conditions and explore the possibilities will depend on whether we have fully developed our ability to think creatively or, more probably, rediscovered it. I love this from the author Paulo Coelho:

> What do I keep from my childhood? I keep my innocence. Innocence is different than to be naïve; innocence is just to have curiosity. I try to see with new and different eyes each day so I am open to life, I am open to new people and I am always discovering new things.

Paulo Coelho is still learning - it's the only way to be.

Bibliography

Allan, Dave, Kingdom, Matt, Murrin, Kris and Rudkin, Daz, ?What If!, *Sticky Wisdom: How to Start a Creative Revolution at Work*, 2002

Allen, David, *Getting Things Done*, 2002

Arden, Paul, *It's Not How Good You Are – It's How Good You Want To Be*, 2003

de Bono, Edward, *I am Right and You are Wrong*, 1991

de Bono, Edward, *Serious Creativity*, 1995

de Bono, Edward, *Six Thinking Hats*, 2000

Brafman, Ori and Beckstron, Rod, *The Starfish and the Spider*, 2008

Carroll, Kevin, *The Red Rubber Ball at Work*, 2008

Collins, Jim, *Good to Great*, 2001

Collins, Jim, *Built to Last*, 2005

Foster, Russell and Kreitzman, Leon, *The Rhythms of Life*, 2005

Friedman, Thomas L., *The World is Flat*, 2007

Gerber, Michael E., *The Emyth Revisited*, 1994

Gladwell, Malcolm, *Blink*, 2006

Godin, Seth, *Permission Marketing*, 2007

Godin, Seth, *Purple Cow*, 2004

Goldman, Robert and Papson, Stephen, *Nike Culture*, 1998

Hall, Doug, *Jump Start Your Business Brain*, 2001

Hoff, Benjamin, *The Tao of Pooh*, 2002

Honda, *Top Talks; Honda's Origin – Thoughts of the Top Guys at Honda Over Time*, 1978

Kahney, Leander, *Inside Steve's Brain*, 2009

Kim, W. Chan and Mauborgne, Renee, *Blue Ocean Strategy*, 2005

Kreitzman, Leon, *The 24 Hour Society*, 1999

Lloyd, Tom, *The Nice Company*, 1990

Lowe, Janet, *Warren Buffett Speaks*, 2007

Lowe, Janet, *Google Speaks: Secrets of the World's Greatest Billionaire Entrepreneurs, Sergey Brin and Larry Page*, 2009

Matsushita, Konosuke, *As I See It*, 1990

Morgan, Adam, *Eating the Big Fish*, 2009

Ogilvy, David, *Ogilvy on Advertising*, 2007

O'Keefe, John, *Business Beyond the Box*, 1998

Peters, Tom, *Re-Imagine*, 2009

Peters, Tom, *The Circle of Innovation*, 1999

Peters, Tom and Waterman, Robert, *In Search of Excellence*, 2004

Popcorn, Faith, *The Popcorn Report*, 1992

Ray, Michael and Myers, Rochelle, *Creativity in Business*, 1998

Schaffer, Robert H., *High Impact Consulting*, 2002

Schmetterer, Bob, *Leap*, 2003

Snyder, Professor Allan, *What Makes a Champion?*, 2002

Steinberger, Michael, *Au Revoir to All That: The Rise and Fall of French Cuisine*, 2009

Toffler, Alvin, *PowerShift*, 1992

Townsend, Robert, *Up the Organisation*, 1970

Vine, David A., *The Google Story*, 2008

Welch, Jack, *Jack: Straight From The Gut*, 2006

Whyte, James, *Bad Thoughts: A Guide to Clear Thinking*, 2003

Wiseman, Edward, *Did You Spot the Gorilla? Spot*, 2004

Index

Also in the *Brilliant* series from Richard Hall ...

A marketing toolbox that will give you the motivation, skills, examples and attitude to carry out the most alluring campaigns around.

Transform your career, save companies and make things happen. Ensure you are brilliant at presenting with this - your secret weapon.

Whatever your level, we'll get you to the next one. It's all about you. Get ready to shine!